SPELLS FOR
MINDFULNESS

SPELLS FOR MINDFULNESS

INCANTATIONS AND CHARMS TO BRING PEACE AND POSITIVITY INTO YOUR LIFE

PAMELA BALL

This edition published in 2019 by Arcturus Publishing Limited
26/27 Bickels Yard, 151–153 Bermondsey Street,
London SE1 3HA

AD006851UK

Printed in the UK

Contents

Introduction

Spells, incantations and charms are all wonderful ways of improving our wellbeing and bringing peace and positive change into our lives, and this book promotes a mindful approach to putting such magical workings into action.

Mindfulness means paying attention to the present moment, to your own thoughts, physical sensations and emotions. Everyone possesses this natural ability, and once mastered, it is ideal for successful spell making. It brings a heightened awareness of what you're experiencing, as well as focusing your attention on what you're thinking, feeling and doing at the time, and what you'd like to have happen next. Importantly, paying more attention to the present moment and the world around you will boost your mental wellbeing.

The good news is that mindfulness can be improved and developed with daily practice, and once you've learned to be in the moment and stop busy thoughts from intruding, you can use spells for an enormous range of purposes – to purify emotions, enhance confidence, create new opportunities and embrace the miracle of each day.

This book is divided into six chapters, each dealing with a particular subject matter or area of life that you'd like to improve: health and healing; love and relationships; wealth and luck; career and decision making; protection; and pot-pourri of spells. The spells cover a wide range of themes, such as how to heal the body, improve self-esteem, ease a broken heart, attract extra money, achieve a dream job, create new business opportunities, cleanse negative energies, protect your pets and create a sacred space in your garden.

Before we start, let us look at what a spell actually is, and how to get the best from your spells.

What is a spell?

In ancient pagan communities, the elders or wise ones had, by their very experience, an awareness of custom and a firm grasp of what had previously worked when trying to gain control over Mother Nature and other powers they did not fully understand. They had access to certain knowledge (and therefore power) that was not readily available to the ordinary individual.

The ancients recognized that words spoken in a certain way according to custom seemed to have more of an effect than those spoken on the spur of the moment. As a consequence, their words would have more power, yet the same words spoken by the uninitiated or those who did not understand did not seem to have the same result.

There are three important aspects when reciting a spell. The first is that words spoken with intensity and passion have a power all of their own. The next is that the speaker also has a power and an energy which, with practice, he or she may learn to use effectively. Third, the forces and powers belonging to that which is 'beyond the human being' also have a tremendous power and are called upon, used or directed for a specific purpose. The use of all three of these aspects gives a very powerful spell indeed.

There are several kinds of spell, each of which requires a different approach.

LOVE SPELLS

When thinking of spells, many people think of love spells – ways of making another person find them attractive and desirable. In theory, love spells should be unconditional, entirely unselfish and free from self-interest. However, most of the time they obviously cannot be so, unless they are performed by a third party, someone outside the longed-for relationship who is totally dispassionate.

To try to influence someone else directly may well go against the ethics of many practitioners and spell makers, although such spells do tend to be the stock-in-trade of many Eastern practitioners. Love spells are often accompanied by gifts or love philtres that are also meant to have an effect on the recipient.

BIDDING SPELLS

These are spells in which the spell maker commands a particular thing to happen, but without the co-operation of those involved. Trying to make someone do something that they do not want to do, or which goes against their natural inclination, obviously requires a great deal of power and energy, and can possibly misfire, causing the originator of the spell a good deal of difficulty.

For this reason, it is wise to preface such spells with words signifying that the outcome will only be in accord with the Greater Good – that is, that in the overall scheme of things, no one will be harmed in any way whatsoever. This ensures that the intent behind the spell is of the purest, and that there is no maliciousness within the practitioner. This means that an able and responsible practitioner must choose their words carefully, even when they are not casting a spell.

One type of bidding spell that is allowable is when a hex or curse is being removed. A hex is a spell that ill-wishes someone, and in many cases binds the recipient in some way. A curse is a spell with a much more generalized effect. To remove negative spells, it is usual to turn them around and send the malign energy back to the person who summoned it in the first place. You simply command the energy to return from whence it came.

BLESSINGS

These might be classified as either prayers or spells, and need passionate concentration to bring peace of mind or healing to the recipient. They hold no danger for the practitioner but are sometimes more difficult to appreciate, since they tend to be more general than other types of magical work. They may be thought of in terms of a positive energy from beyond the practitioner being channelled towards a specific purpose.

Saying Grace is a form of blessing preceded by an offer of praise and a prayer of thankfulness, an acknowledgement of a gift. The food is enhanced by the act, and the blessing is given by drawing on the power vested in the knowledgeable expert. Thus, one practitioner may call on the Nature Gods, whereas another might call on the power of Jesus Christ.

HEALING SPELLS AND CHARMS

Within this type of spell, it is wise to go beyond the presenting symptoms and to ask for healing on all levels of existence –

physical, mental and spiritual – because the practitioner may not have the knowledge or correct information to enable him or her to diagnose a condition correctly. The natural energies and specific vibrations are enhanced by invocations, incantations and blessings wherever appropriate.

Frequently, objects such as crystals are charged with energy and power to focus healing or other energies in a quite specific way, often to remind the patient's body of its own inbuilt ability to heal itself.

INVOCATIONS

These call on what is believed to be the ultimate source of power, which differs from spell to spell. Quite literally, an invocation calls up that power and asks for permission to use its influence for a stated purpose. Meddling with this power and calling up negative forces is extremely unwise and foolish.

Spells for selfish personal power or to gain power over others will often backfire on the unwary, and may cause damage to whoever casts them. Invocations of positive forces can do no harm. The results, however, can sometimes be highly disconcerting due to the sheer energy created, although the eventual outcome may be good.

THE INCANTATION

This type of spell prepares the magical worker and his or her helpers for further work by heightening their awareness. It does not set out to call up the powers, but appeals to gods, goddesses, powers of nature and so on for help.

Chanting, prayer and hymns are in many ways incantations, particularly when the intent is stated with some passion. An incantation is often very beautiful and rhythmic. Music has always been an efficient way of heightening awareness and altering states of consciousness.

Types of spell making

There are many different ways in which a spell can be made, from working with particular colours or burning a candle to using knot magic or wearing special devices such as amulets or charms. The following are the main types of spell making.

ELEMENTAL

In this particular type of magic, the elements of fire, earth, air and water are given their own directional focus to create added power and give extra energy to your spells. You will no doubt find that you tend to favour one particular direction, but you should learn to use them all.

COLOUR

Perhaps the simplest form of magic is that involving colour, and this method of working is also used in conjunction with various other forms of magic. Colour can enhance, alter and completely change moods and emotions, and can therefore be used to represent our chosen goal. At its simplest, it can be used alone, or used in dressing an altar. We give some colour correspondences on pages 35–6.

HERBAL

Magic involving herbs is often used alongside many other forms of magic. Used as talismans and amulets – for example in a pouch or bag – herbs become protective. Alternatively, the oil from herbs can also be used in candle magic. There are many different types of herbs available for use in this way. Each one has its own specific purpose, but frequently it is used along with many other herbs and oils to produce a desired result.

CANDLE

Early humans discovered the ability to control fire, and candle magic is one of the oldest forms of spell making, as well as one of the simplest. Using candles to symbolize ourselves and our beliefs means that we have access to a power beyond ourselves. Candle magic also forms an effective back-up for most other forms of magical working.

CRYSTAL

Every stone or gem has its own particular attribute which can be used in magic. Crystals are used extensively in healing because of the vibrational impact they can have, and in fact they lend themselves to the enhancement of almost any spell or magical working. Even ordinary stones have their own power and can be used as repositories for all sorts of energies and powers.

KNOT

Working partly with the principle of binding and also with that of weaving (traditionally a female intuitive occupation), knot magic comes under the category of a bidding spell. It utilizes ribbon, rope, string, yarn or anything that can be knotted or plaited to signify our aspirations. It can be performed in conjunction with many of the other forms of magic. The techniques of colour, form and use of energies are all employed in its practice.

REPRESENTATIONAL

This type of magic involves using an object that represents something or someone for whom you are working the spell. It helps in concentrating the energy and visualizing the desire and the end result. Representational objects should never be used for negative purposes.

SYMBOLIC

In this system, different symbols (rather than objects) are used to represent various ideas, people or goals. The symbols can be personal to you, or alternatively you can use Tarot cards, runes, Hebrew letters or numerology symbols. You will often need to use symbolic magic in your magical workings, and will soon develop your own preferred symbols.

TALISMANS, AMULETS AND CHARMS

These devices use all the other forms of magic in their formation. They are 'charged' (given power) magically, and are usually worn or carried on the person for protection or good luck. Many are worn around the neck, perhaps as jewellery, or carried in a pouch, and they may incorporate crystals, herbs or other magical objects. There are many types of these objects, and you will gradually learn to differentiate between them.

Equipment and ingredients

When performing your spells and magical workings, you will probably find that you tend to use some equipment and ingredients more than others. The pages that follow provide details about the tools, candles, crystals, herbs, incenses and oils that are most commonly used.

TOOLS

ALTAR Objects may include candleholders, flower vases, crystals etc that do not necessarily have a specific magical use of their own, but are used to create an ambience. You can dedicate them to the purpose at hand by presenting them to your chosen deity. Some spell makers may prefer to work according to their preferred tradition, such as Celtic, Norse, Graeco-Roman or Wiccan. Here are some of the main tools you may need:

ATHAME By tradition, an athame is a ceremonial knife used especially in the performing of spells. It is not used for cutting of herbs and so on. Its role is purely ceremonial – for example, indicating the four quarters or directions. By tradition, it should be of the best and purest metal available. Its handle is usually black and sometimes carved with magical designs and symbols. Many experienced magical practitioners consider that the most powerful athame is one that has been inherited.

BESOM is a different name for a broom, and is particularly associated with the easily recognizable so-called 'witch's broom' of old. A particularly personal tool, it is often made specifically for the practitioner, from twigs from the tree of his/her choice. It is usually kept specifically to be used in the sacred space or circle – this time for cleansing – and is also used both symbolically and spiritually.

BOLINE This is a knife traditionally used in cutting plants, herbs, wands and other objects for magical workings. It is not the same as the athame, which is purely ceremonial, but is akin to the gardener's pruning knife as a useful, practical tool. It often has a white handle and a curved blade. It is consecrated, because this is a way of honouring its purpose.

BURIN This is a sharp, pointed instrument used for inscribing candles and objects with symbols, words and pictures in order to make spells more effective. In many ways, it is more effective than the boline or athame, and is seen more as an instrument that pierces the surface of an object rather than cutting it.

CANDLES are such an integral part of a spell maker's work that they have become a whole branch of magic all their own. They represent the element of fire, but also light. As explained in more detail later, various colours bring different qualities to magical workings, and they are an important part of any ritual.

CAULDRON Because cauldrons were easily disguised as cooking utensils in olden days, most people today tend to think of a cauldron as a large cast-iron pot. There has lately been a return to original materials, but nowadays they can be made of almost anything. A cauldron is often of a size that can stand on an altar or in a sacred space. It is used mainly as a container for herbs, candles and other magical objects.

CHALICE Used as a ceremonial drinking vessel, a chalice is sometimes made from precious metal, although it can also be made from glass. An elegant object, the chalice will usually be beautifully decorated with elaborate designs – which may have magical significance – or jewels and gemstones.

PAPER We often need to write our wishes or aims down when making spells, and it is a good idea to have some paper ready prepared. Parchment type is best, but heavier, good-quality paper is also good. You consecrate it by holding it for a short period in the smoke from your favourite incense.

PEN AND INK Traditionally, quill pens were used for writing spells and incantations, but if you can't find a quill, then use the best pen you can afford. Try to keep it just for magical work, and consecrate it by passing it carefully over the top of a candle or through incense. Also buy a good-quality ink and, if not already formulated for magical purposes, consecrate that in the same way. Neither pen nor ink should be used for any other purposes.

PENTACLE This is a shallow dish that is usually inscribed with a pentagram – a five-pointed star. It is used as a 'power point' for consecrating other objects such as amulets, tools, or water or wine in a chalice.

PESTLE AND MORTAR These are so symbolic of the union of God and Goddess that they deserve a special mention within the use of magical tools. Mainly used to prepare herbal mixtures and incenses, they can also become part of your altar furniture once they have been consecrated.

SCRYING TOOLS The practice known as scrying is the use of certain channelling tools that are consecrated before use – such as crystals, mirrors, coloured water, runes etc – to try to gain an insight into external events. Any object can be used for scrying, although usually they are reflective and they employ the arts of concentration and contemplation.

STAFF This is used very frequently by practitioners today, particularly those of the Druidic persuasion. Longer than a wand, it has the same attributes and uses. A staff is deliberately fashioned for the practitioner from wood taken from a sacred tree such as oak, hawthorn or hazelnut.

WAND This should be no longer than the forearm, and is often made from sacred wood. Since a wand is a very personal object it should be chosen with great care, and equally carefully attuned to your own energies. It cannot be used magically until it has been consecrated.

CANDLES

We have already mentioned candle magic, but since candles are such an important part of magical working, they deserve a special section of their own. They should be chosen carefully with regard to type and colour, depending on the purpose of the spell. It is often better to use your intuition when choosing the type of candle, although for ease of reference, below is a list of the principal types. There are other types available, but those listed here are the most suitable for magical working.

TABLE CANDLES are the most easily available type, and are ideal for many of the spells in this book. They usually burn for between 6 to 8 hours and do need to be properly seated in suitable candlesticks. All colours can be used, but they should not be dipped, except in exceptional circumstances, and should be of the best quality possible. It is sensible to keep a ready supply to hand.

PILLAR This is a free-standing candle. It is usually in the shape of a simple pillar, although it can sometimes be made in other shapes that can be used as part of the spell, e.g. heart shapes for love spells. This type of candle is best burned on a flat holder, since it usually takes some time to burn out.

TAPER This is tall and thin, and needs a particularly stable candle holder. Taper candles are either made in a mould, or by the traditional method of dipping a length of wick into hot molten white or coloured wax. For magical purposes, they should be coloured all the way through. They can often be used when a quick result is required. Since they are quite fragile, you need to be careful not to break them when anointing them.

TEALIGHTS are excellent for when a candle must be left to burn out, but they are less easy to anoint with essential oils. Poured in small metal pots like small votives, they are normally used in oil burners or specially made tealight holders. Depending on their size, they usually burn for approximately 4 hours.

VOTIVE CANDLES are specially designed as offerings to carry prayers to whichever deity you honour. As the wax melts, the glass holder can become hot, so take care when using them. They are designed to be long-burning, usually from 1–7 days.

Things to remember when choosing a candle:

✴ Candles used for magic should always be virgin (unused) at the start of the working, unless you have deliberately cleared them of past influences. Using candles that have been previously lit can have a detrimental effect on your spell. They may have picked up influences from previous use.

☽ Charge your candle before use. This can be done by anointing it with oils associated with the magic you intend to perform, or by simply touching it and filling it with your own energy.

● The oils used in the anointing of your candle should, where possible, always be natural fragrances. While charging the candle, smooth from top to bottom when drawing energy towards you, and bottom to top when sending energy outwards. Particularly when anointing candles for altar use, anoint from the middle to the top and from the middle to the bottom to signify the union of spiritual and physical realms.

If you enjoy craftwork, it is a great idea to make your own candles for magical use. A whole art in itself, you infuse candles with your own energy as you work, and thus increase the magical potency of the candle many times over. It is relatively easy to make your own candles: simply heat the wax until it is liquid, then pour it into a mould that is threaded with a wick. The wax should be left to cool, after which the mould can be removed. Oils and colours can be added for extra potency.

Many different colours are used in candle magic. The most common ones, along with their key associations and purposes, are listed on pages 35–6. You may not wish to use black candles because of their association with the darker side of magic. If so, dark grey is a good substitute.

CRYSTALS

There are many crystals that can be used in magical workings. This is a brief list of some well-known ones that you may like to try. The list also gives some of the correspondences that are most often used in healing spells in particular. This is because a crystal can be charged with healing energy. Many people do not wish it to be known that they are using healing energy on behalf of others, and using a crystal is an easy way of doing so unobtrusively. As you become more practised in spell making, you will discover for yourself that certain crystals resonate for you more than others.

AGATE A member of the quartz family, this is a general healer, especially good for self-esteem.

AMETHYST A crystalline quartz, this helps with creative thinking and is a protector against blood diseases, grief, neuralgia and insomnia. It is also said to deal with drunkenness.

AQUAMARINE A clear silicate, this is good for the eyes and helps against nerve, throat, liver and stomach troubles.

BLOODSTONE A dark green quartz flecked with red jasper, this strengthens the will to do good.

CARNELIAN A translucent red or orange, this makes the voice strong and is helpful when dealing with rheumatism, depression and neuralgia.

CITRINE A form of crystalline quartz, this may bring greater control over the emotions, and also help blood circulation.

EMERALD This dark green precious stone is a silicate. It improves the intellect and memory, and may help with insomnia.

GARNET This is the name given to a group of gemstones of varying composition, ranging from a deep blood-red through to orange. It protects against depression and helps with self-confidence and self-esteem.

JADE Nephrite jade is a silicate with a green colour. It is beneficial when dealing with kidney complaints.

JASPER This is a mixed type of quartz that can occur in various colours. It improves the sense of smell and helps liver, kidney and epileptic problems.

LAPIS LAZULI A mixture of minerals of a deep blue colour, this often contains particles of 'fool's gold'. This is an ancient stone that is useful for heart and vascular conditions.

MOONSTONE A silicate, this stone has a milky sheen, with the best stones containing a blueish colour. It gives inspiration and enhances the emotions.

ONYX This type of agate is often coloured jet-black and is highly polished. It helps with concentration and is an important healing agent in certain ear diseases.

OPAL A hydrated silica, this helps in lung conditions.

ROCK-CRYSTAL A colourless pure quartz, this is an important healing stone and also helps to improve intuitive powers.

ROSE QUARTZ A translucent quartz, this sparks the imagination and calms the emotions.

RUBY A precious stone, this is an oxide of aluminium that is coloured red by chromium. It improves mental ability.

SAPPHIRE This has the same composition as ruby, but is usually a rich blue colour due to traces of iron and titanium. The stone of friendship and love, it gives devotion, faith and imagination.

SMOKY QUARTZ An attractive crystalline with a smoky grey to black colour, this is used to give good luck.

TIGER'S EYE A quartz mineral, this is worn for clearer thinking.

TOURMALINE A complex silicate, this attracts inspiration, goodwill and friendship.

TURQUOISE An opaque stone given its blue-green colour by copper, this is a good protector, and is therefore an ideal stone to give as a gift.

HERBS

Most magical practices make use of herbs in various ways, usually in rituals and magical workings. Often they are used as incense in which they are crushed and powdered, or as oils. Their properties mean that they create a type of forcefield that intensifies the vibration needed. Additionally, when the practitioner calls upon the power of the gods and spirits, the herbs become even more effective.

Simply having particular herbs in your sacred space or keeping them about your person is sufficient to begin the process of enhancing the area or your personal vibration. You can use them in incense and dedicate them to the appropriate elements and deities. Many of the herbs in this book can be obtained from a good herbalist, although for those of you who are truly interested, it would be worthwhile creating a small herb garden or growing them on your windowsill.

Here are some of the most popular reasons for using herbs in spell making:

PROTECTION Such herbs guard against physical and psychic attacks, injury, accidents and entities such as wicked spirits. They usually offer protection in a general sort of way.

LOVE The vibration of these herbs is such that they can help you meet new people, overcome shyness and let others know that you are open to new relationships. They put out a particular vibration so that people who are interested will answer the call. The safest way to use them is to accept that several people may be attracted to you, and you will then be able to make an informed choice.

FIDELITY According to tradition, some herbs and plants can be used to ensure fidelity. You do have to have a firm belief that you have a right to another's devotion before imposing your will on them. Using a spell for fidelity amounts to a binding spell, and you must make allowances for the person's own integrity. It is unwise and sometimes unhelpful to both parties to hold anyone in a relationship against their will.

HEALING Many herbs have healing properties that can help from both a physical and a magical viewpoint. A practitioner working from both viewpoints can be of tremendous help in managing illness. However, always remember to advise anyone you work with to seek qualified medical assistance. Never allow yourself to be drawn into being a substitute for medical help.

HEALTH Not only the smell of herbs and plants but also their vibration can help to prevent illness and restore good health. So, if you are prone to illness, carry health herbs with you and make sure they are always as fresh as possible.

LUCK Defined as the knack of being in the right place at the right time, luck also involves being able to act on instinct. Luck herbs can help you create your own good fortune. Once you have such a foundation, you can build upon it.

MONEY It is sometimes easier to visualize the outcome of having money, i.e. what you are going to spend your money on, rather than visualizing actual money coming to you. Certain herbs create an environment in which financial windfalls can happen. They enable the creation of the means to fulfil your needs – perhaps a gift, a pay rise or some such event.

Since herbs are used so extensively in this book, here is a list of some of the main uses and more important herbs:

ATTRACTING MEN: Jasmine, Juniper (dried berries worn as a charm), Lavender, Lemon Verbena, Lovage, Orris Root, Patchouli.

ATTRACTING WOMEN: Henbane, Holly, Juniper (dried berries worn as a charm), Lemon Verbena, Lovage, Orris Root, Patchouli.

BANISHING: Hyssop, Lilac, St John's Wort.

CLEANSING: Cinnamon, Clove, Lovage (powdered root), Pine, Thyme (in baths), Vervain (of sacred spaces).

COURAGE: Basil, Garlic, Mullein, Nettle, St John's Wort, Thyme, Wormwood, Yarrow.

EXORCISM: Angelica, Basil, Birch, Frankincense, Juniper, Garlic, St John's Wort.

FERTILITY: Acorns, Geranium, Hawthorn, Mandrake, Orange (dried and powdered peel), Pine, Poppy, Sage, Sunflower (seeds).

FRIENDSHIP: Lemon, Rose, Passion Flower.

GOOD FORTUNE: Ash (leaves), Heather, Nutmeg, Rose, Vetivert.

HAPPINESS: Anise, Catnip, Lily of the Valley, Marjoram, Saffron.

HARMONY: Hyacinth, Heliotrope, Lilac, Meadowsweet.

HEALING: Aloe, Ash, Chamomile, Cinnamon, Comfrey, Eucalyptus, Fennel, Garlic, Hops, Marjoram, Mint, Nettle, Pine, Rosemary, Saffron, Sage, Sandalwood, Thyme, Yarrow.

HEX BREAKING: Chilli Pepper, Galangal, Vetivert.

LOVE: Apple, Balm of Gilead, Basil, Caraway, Catnip, Coriander, Cowslip, Dill, Gardenia, Ginger, Ginseng, Honeysuckle, Jasmine, Lavender, Linden, Marigold, Marjoram, Meadowsweet, Mistletoe, Myrtle, Rose, Rosemary, Valerian, Vervain, Violet (mixed with Lavender), Yarrow.

LUCK: Apple, Ash (leaves), Hazel, Holly (for newlyweds), Ivy (for newlyweds), Mint, Rose, Rowan, Vervain, Violet (flowers).

LUST: Cinnamon, Lemongrass, Nettle, Rosemary, Violet.

MEDITATION: Chamomile, Elecampane, Frankincense, Vervain.

MENTAL POWERS: Caraway, Lily of the Valley, Rosemary, Vanilla, Walnut.

MONEY: Chamomile, Cinnamon, Clove, Comfrey, Fennel, Ginger, Mint, Poppy, Vervain.

PEACE: Aloe, Chamomile, Gardenia, Lavender, Myrtle, Violet.

POWER: Carnation, Cinnamon, Ginger, Rosemary, Rowan.

PROSPERITY: Acorn, Almond, Ash, Basil, Benzoin, Honeysuckle.

Note: There are so many herbs suitable for the next three categories (Protection, Psychic Powers and Purification) and the choice is such a personal one that we have included only a few suggestions. Your own further research will very much enhance your magical workings.

PROTECTION: Aloe, Angelica (root), Anise, Balm of Gilead, Basil, Bay Laurel, Black Pepper, Caraway, Chamomile, Dill (for children), Dragon's Blood, Fennel, Garlic, Hawthorn, Holly, Hyssop, Lavender, Mandrake, Meadowsweet, Mistletoe, Mugwort, Nettle, Periwinkle, Rose, Rosemary, Rowan, Sage, St John's Wort, Sandalwood, Vervain, Witch Hazel, Wormwood.

PSYCHIC POWERS: Ash (leaves), Bay Laurel, Bay (leaves), Cinnamon, Cowslip, Elecampane, Eyebright, Hyssop, Lavender, Marigold, Mugwort, Nutmeg, Rose, Thyme, Wormwood, Yarrow.

PURIFICATION: Anise, Betony, Cinquefoil, Dragon's Blood, Frankincense, Hyssop, Lavender, Lemon, Oak Leaves, Pine, Rosemary, Rue, Sandalwood, Thyme, Valerian, Vervain.

SUCCESS: Cinnamon, Ginger, Lemon Balm, Rowan.

SLEEP: Catnip, Hops, Lavender, Thyme, Valerian, Vervain.

SPIRITUALITY: Cinnamon, Clover, Frankincense, Myrrh, Sandalwood.

WISDOM: Peach (fruit), Sage, Sunflower.

INCENSE

As well as making use of herbs as plants, for decorations and for healing, their most important use in magic was – and still is – in incense. Incense symbolizes the element of air and the spiritual realms, and has been part of ritual use by occultists and priests alike for thousands of years. Nowadays, granular incense, with its basis of resins and gums, sweet-smelling woods and herbs, is usually preferred for magical workings or ritual worship. It has a magic all of its own. For this reason, a good incense burner will be one of your most important pieces of equipment. You should choose this carefully – not just for its aesthetic sense, but because it is vital that the incense is allowed to burn properly.

Egypt became especially renowned for its high standard of blending and the use of ritual incense. There was a particular class of incense – which is still available today – called Khyphi. It required magical techniques and the finest ingredients for its manufacture. Some incenses were mind-altering and could produce trance-like states in users.

For short spells, joss sticks work very well, although they are not to everyone's taste. Dhoop, or incense cones as they are known, are another way of using the same material. By far the best method is to burn the granular type on a charcoal disc that is lit and placed in a fireproof receptacle. The incense is then piled onto the concave surface and allowed to do its work. You should dispose of the discs very carefully, dousing them with water and ensuring they are no longer hot. You might like to bury what remains of the incense as an offering to the Earth.

Many of the herbs we have already encountered are suitable for incense, if you wish to make your own. You should choose your correspondences carefully, according to your spell. You will soon find out through experimentation what works for you.

When blending your own granular incense, it is important to use a pestle and mortar to grind and mix all the ingredients together properly. You may wish to consecrate your pestle and mortar first. Granular incense usually consists of a base of incense gums to which are added the woods and herbs of choice before the mixture is blended using fragrant oils.

BLENDING GRANULAR INCENSE

✦ When blending, first grind the gum resins (such as gum Arabic or benzoin) until the granules are like granulated sugar.

⟫ Add the woods, herbs and spices, all of which should have been finely ground and thoroughly blended together.

● Then add the essential oils, one drop at a time, and mix well. The blending of the incense is an important part of the process, both from the perspective of the synergy of the ingredients and the personal energy you add to the incense.

◀ At this point you might like to dedicate the incense to the purpose intended, saying perhaps simply:

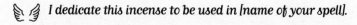 *I dedicate this incense to be used in [name of your spell].*

⚡ Place the incense mixture in a strong polythene bag (so that it retains its pungency), then put it into a clean jar sealed with a screw-top lid.

◀ Do not use the incense for at least 24 hours, to enable the perfumes and qualities to blend properly.

◀ Don't forget to label the jar, noting the ingredients and the date you made the blend. It is also a good idea to note the intention or purpose for which the incense was made.

♥ Make your incense in small quantities so that it does not lose its potency.

When making your incense, you may like to follow the example of herbalists of old, who gathered their herbs in tune with the cycles of life and planetary correspondences. Even though you may have to use store-bought herbs, the more you are able to work with the correspondences (see pages 20–2) and think about timing, the more effective your spells or rituals will be.

OILS

Particularly when space is at a premium, oils are an easy way of using plants and herbs in magical workings. The following are some oils that should be part of every magical practitioner's way of working. All of them are simple to acquire and, if stored according to directions, they will last for some time – so even though the initial expense may seem prohibitive, they are actually well worth the cost.

CINNAMON With its warm vibration, this brings love from higher realms, transforming sadness into happiness.

CLARY SAGE lifts the spirit and links with eternal wisdom, teaching us to be content with what we have and that most problems arise in our imagination.

FRANKINCENSE holds some of the wisdom of the universe. Able to cleanse the most negative of influences, frankincense works far beyond the auric field, affecting the very subtle realms of energy and adapting the spiritual state. It is sometimes called 'olibanum'.

GERANIUM resonates with Mother Earth and all that is feminine. It comforts, opens our hearts and heals pain. It typifies the archetypal energy of Goddess culture. Its energy is transformational, and as such, it must always be used with respect.

JASMINE provides us with access to a greater understanding of the spirit. It is said that jasmine brings the angelic kingdom within our reach. It gives understanding and acceptance of the true meaning of spirituality.

LAVENDER is caring and nurturing. It will not allow negative emotion to remain present, bringing about healing by allowing heavenly energies to come close to the physical.

MYRRH brings the realization that we no longer need to carry our burdens, releasing them from deep within and allowing us to let go when the time is right. When combined with other oils, it both enhances and is enhanced by them.

NEROLI is one of the most precious essential oils, its vibration being one of the highest. It brings self-recognition as it allows a new perspective that helps us to develop unconditional love.

NUTMEG When the spirit is affected by disappointment, emotional pain and displacement, nutmeg works to bring hopes, dreams and prayers back into focus.

ROSE ABSOLUT Said to be the perfume of the guardians or messengers who guide us in times of need, this is a fragrance that allows us to access the divine mysteries. It is associated with the true needs of the human heart.

ROSEMARY reminds us of our purpose and our own spiritual journey, and encourages confidence and clarity of purpose. It cleanses the aura.

SANDALWOOD allows us to make contact with divine beings and brings us into balance with the cosmos. It clarifies our strength of conviction.

YLANG YLANG balances the spirit so that we can be open to pleasures of the physical realm while still appreciating spiritual passions. Used magically, it achieves a balanced manifestation

In essence, spells can be as simple or as complex as one wishes to make them. Which you use and what you wish to do depend on your own preference and, indeed, the intention of the spell. We are extremely lucky today to have many choices available, many disciplines having been tried and tested through long experience. It used to be thought that the spell maker should stick to one discipline and become proficient at that, being initiated only into their own craft. As knowledge expands, however, and we realize that there are similarities in the results that can be produced, it can do no harm to make the effort to understand other people's ways of working and to incorporate these into our own practice.

Preparations for spell making

Several processes become automatic when preparing for spell work, from bathing and choosing what to wear to setting up and consecrating your altar.

Ritual bathing

Some magical workings require you to take a ritual bath that cleanses, purifies and clarifies your energy so that you are able to get the best results possible. Many practitioners prefer to take a ritual bath before performing any magical workings.

As you mix your salts into the bath, bless the water and charge it with your intent – be that a particular magical working, a relaxing evening or a successful meeting. The candles used in this ritual can be in the colours of the elements or those most appropriate to your purpose; for example, pink (tranquillity), blue (wisdom), green (self-awareness) and red (passion). For spiritual matters, use purple.

YOU WILL NEED
- ✦ HOMEMADE BATH SALTS
- ☽ VOTIVE CANDLES ACCORDING TO YOUR NEED
- ● LARGE WHITE CANDLE
- ◐ ESSENTIAL OIL TO REMOVE NEGATIVITY (E.G. ROSEMARY)
- ⚡ LARGE GLASS OF MINERAL WATER OR JUICE

METHOD
Anoint the large white candle with the essential oil and ask for positivity, health and happiness as you do so.

Do the same with the votive candles according to your need. If you wish, you may inscribe a symbol to represent your purpose on each candle.

Run your bath and mix in the bath salts.

Light the candles, first the white one followed by the votives.

Place the latter safely around the bath.

The white candle should be placed wherever you feel is safest.

You have now created a sacred space for yourself.

Lie back and enjoy your bath, and at some point drink your water or juice, visualizing your whole system being cleansed inside as well as out.

Before you get out of the bath, thank the water deities for this opportunity to prepare thoroughly for the new energies available to you.

If you are to perform a magical working, keep your mind focused on that intent.

When you have finished your bath, snuff out the candles.

Making your own bath salts

Commercial bath salts will do absolutely nothing on an esoteric level – they have too many chemical additives and artificial perfumes – so it's a nice touch to make your own using single essential oils, blends and/or herbs. The fact that you have mixed them yourself means they are infused with your own vibration and will therefore work on a very subtle level. Matching your bath salt perfume to your incense perfume also does wonders for your inner self.

YOU WILL NEED
- ✦ 3 PARTS EPSOM SALTS
- ☽ 2 PARTS BAKING SODA
- ● 1 PART ROCK SALT OR BORAX
- ◗ BOWL
- ⚡ ESSENTIAL OILS IN YOUR CHOSEN PERFUMES
- ◗ HANDFUL OF HERBS (OPTIONAL)
- ◖ NATURAL FOOD COLOURING

METHOD

Mix the first three ingredients thoroughly in the bowl. Use your hands, as this will enable you to imbue the salts with your own energy.

This is your basic mixture, and can be perfumed or coloured in any way that you please.

Note: When using a blend of essential oils, it is wise to mix them first. This allows the synergy between the oils to develop.

Add your colouring first, then mix to your satisfaction, then follow with your oil or blend, one drop at a time.

Be generous with the oils, since the salts will absorb a surprising amount without you realizing.

As with all oils and perfumes, your nose is the best judge – there is no right or wrong amount.

Add the herbs (if using) to the mixture and combine thoroughly.

When you wish to use your salts, add approximately 2 tablespoons to a full bathtub and mix well.

Clothing and jewellery

There is no limit to what can be worn. Some suggest white robes with black cords or vice versa, while others simply suggest that you be comfortable in what you wear. Many people will spend a great deal of time, energy and effort on fashioning suitable robes. The idea is that you should leave behind the ordinary, mundane world when working magically, so turn off phones, put away keys, and remove money and other objects from your pockets, and so on.

Magical jewellery – such as the pentagram, ankh or rings with magical symbols or significance – are often worn, although they are by no means essential. Many people prefer not to wear watches, since time is considered irrelevant.

Poppets

A poppet is a small doll or figurine made from wood, paper, material or clay. It is shaped roughly in human form and is primarily used for magic spells. Originating from West African belief systems, poppets can be used to represent and help either the maker of the doll or another person.

You should only make a poppet of someone else if they have given permission, such as when you wish to help or heal someone. To make a poppet without permission or for inappropriate reasons creates the wrong energy vibration and introduces a negativity into your magical workings.

Making a poppet

When you are making a poppet, it is good to have taken a ritual purification bath beforehand (see pages 26–7), or alternatively to have meditated on whether the use of a poppet is appropriate at this time and how best to make use of it. This is to ensure that, as far as possible, you have removed any subjective feelings and emotions about the subject and are acting only as the creator of the object. You need to know that you are merely the channel for the energy that is being used.

YOU WILL NEED
✦ PAPER OR CARD (TO ACT AS A TEMPLATE)
⟡ SOFT MATERIAL SUCH AS FELT OR COTTON
● NEEDLE AND THREAD
◗ STRAW, PAPER OR COTTON WOOL
⚡ HERBS FOR THE RITUAL YOU ARE PERFORMING
  (IF APPROPRIATE)

METHOD
Draw the outline of a simple human figure on the paper or card, then cut it out. It should ideally be at least 4 in (10 cm) high.

Fold the material in two, then place the template on it.

Cut around the template.

Sew the figures together, leaving a small area open.

Turn the figure inside out, so the stitches are on the inside.

Stuff the figure with the straw, paper, cotton wool or herbs. You can personalize the poppet by adding a lock of hair to the filling.

You can also use buttons for eyes, or draw on facial features if you wish.

Finish sewing the material together.

Your poppet is now ready for use. Do not destroy it when you have finished with it – either give it to the person whom it represents or bury it safely in the earth.

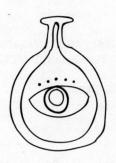

Consecrating your sacred space

If you are going to be carrying out a fair number of rituals or spells, you will need a sacred space or altar, along with various other altar furnishings. Whether this is indoors or outside does not matter. To set up your sacred space and/or altar indoors, it should preferably be in a quiet place in the home, where it will not be disturbed and where candles can be burned safely.

✦ The space first needs to be dedicated to the purpose of magical working. You can do this by first brushing the area clean with an ordinary brush, concentrating your thoughts on cleansing the space as you work physically to bring this about. You should also mentally cleanse the space three times, imagining doing it once for the physical world, once for the emotional space, and once spiritually.

☽ If you wish, you may sprinkle the whole area with water, then salt (which represents the Earth). You might perhaps also burn incense such as jasmine or frankincense to clear the atmosphere. Think of your sacred space as somewhere you would entertain an honoured guest in your home – you would wish the room to be as welcoming as possible. You can use a besom to keep the sacred space clear.

● If you travel a lot or are pushed for space, you might dedicate a tray or special piece of wood or china for ceremonial working. This, along with your candles and incense, can then be kept together in a small box or suitcase. Otherwise, you could dedicate a table dedicated to the purpose. Ideally, you should not need to pack up each time.

◗ You will also need a 'fine cloth' – the best you can afford – to cover the surface. Place the cloth on your chosen surface, then spend some quiet time just thinking about its purpose. If you wish, you may keep different cloths for different purposes, or perhaps have one basic cloth that is then 'dressed' with the appropriate colour for each ritual.

Setting up your altar

To turn your dressed table into a proper altar, you will need the following objects:

✦ Two candles with candle holders. You might like to think of one as representing the female principle and the other as the male. In addition, you may choose candles in a colour suitable for the ritual or spell you are working.

☽ An incense holder and incense suitable for your particular spell.

● A representation of the deity or deities you prefer to work with. An image of a goddess, for instance, could be anything from a statue of the Chinese Goddess of Compassion, Kuan Yin, to seashells, chalices, bowls, or certain stones that symbolize the womb or motherhood.

◗ A small vase for flowers or fresh herbs.

Consecrating altar objects

If you are not using completely new objects on your altar, you should cleanse them before you dedicate them to your purpose. Treat them in the same way as you would your crystals: soak them overnight in salt water to remove anyone else's vibrations, then stand them in sunshine (or moonshine) for at least 12 hours to charge them with the appropriate energy.

✦ When you are ready, hold each object and allow your own energy to flow into it, followed by the energy of your idea of Ultimate Power. In this way, you make a very strong link between yourself, the object and the Ultimate. Ask this Power to bless the object and any working you may do with it and perceive yourself truly as a medium or channel for the energy.

☽ Hopefully, each time you use any of the objects you will immediately be able to reinforce that link rather than having to re-establish it – a bit like a refrain continually running in the background. Place the objects on your altar in whichever way you feel is right for you.

Casting a circle

If appropriate, create and caste a circle so that it includes yourself and your altar. This magic circle defines the ritual area, holds in personal power and shuts out all distractions and negative energies.

✦ Purify yourself first. You can do this by meditating or taking a ritual bath. Try to keep the water flowing, possibly by leaving the bath plug half in, or by having a shower. This reinforces the idea of washing away any impurities. (You may scent your bath water with your selection of a sacred or special herb or oil.) Ideally, your towel, if you choose to use one, should be clean and used only for the purpose of your ritual bath.

⟩ Wear something special. This sets spell making apart from everyday confusion. You could add a pretty scarf or a throw in the correct colour for your working.

● Decide on the extent of your circle, which should be formed in front of your altar. Purify this space by sprinkling the area with water followed by salt. Both of these should have been blessed beforehand.

◖ Sit quietly for as long as you can inside the area that will become your circle.

⚡ Imagine a circle of light surrounding you. This light could be white, blue or purple. If you are in a hurry and cannot purify and cleanse fully, reinforce the circle of light by visualizing it suffused with the appropriate colour for your working.

◗ Circle the light around, above and below you in a clockwise direction, like the representation of an atom. Feel it as a sphere or cone of power. Sense the power. Remember to leave a 'doorway' through which your magic energy may exit. You should always feel warm and peaceful within your circle.

◖ Use a personal chant or form of words according to your own belief system to consecrate your circle. Banish all evil and negative energy, forbidding anything harmful to enter your space. Remember, you are always safe within your circle if you command it to be so.

♥ If appropriate, invite the gods and goddesses to attend your circle and magical working.

✦ Relax and be happy.

If you wish, you can use objects on the ground to show the boundaries of the circle, such as candles, crystals, cord, stones, flowers or incense. The circle is formed from personal power, which may be felt and visualized as streaming from the body to form a bubble of mist or a circle of light. You can use the athame (ritual dagger) or your hands to direct this power.

The cardinal points of the compass may be denoted with lit candles, often white or purple. Alternatively, place a green candle at the north point of the circle, a yellow candle at the east, a red candle at the south, and a blue candle at the west. The altar stands in the centre of the circle, facing north in the direction of power.

Consecrating your tools

Most magical traditions make use of the familiar magical elements of earth, air, fire and water. Some traditions have specific tools that are important to them. There is also a fifth magical element: that of spirit. The simplest consecration that can be made is to offer each of the objects to spirit so that they may be used for the best purpose possible. You can specifically dedicate any tool using a short invocation such as:

> *I dedicate this magical tool to the purpose for which it is intended.*

You can, of course, be as creative with your speech as you desire. Anything else that is done will be according to the traditions of your own belief.

Regarding your tools (see pages 13–15), when you first purchase them or have them made, cleanse them before use, then dedicate them by filling them with your own energy as you did with your altar objects. You might also offer them to your appropriate deity.

Colour

With practice, colour is something that you will use as a natural adjunct in your magical workings. It can be used in your robes or to dress your altar, or in your candles to represent the vibration you wish to introduce. By and large, the colours you choose for your workings need to be appropriate for your spell's intention or purpose. Some simple colour symbolism is listed below.

SILVER AND WHITE Silver is almost always associated with the Lunar Goddesses and workings with the Moon. White symbolizes purity, chastity and spirituality, and is said to contain within it all the other colours, so always use white if you have nothing else available. Also use it when you want focus and a protective influence.

PURPLE, INDIGO AND VIOLET are the Royal colours, and are therefore associated with wisdom and vision, dignity and fame. They are often used when honouring the Goddess in her aspect of Crone and the God as King, according to some traditions of magic. These colours command respect and promote psychic and mental healing.

SKY BLUE signifies communication in all its forms, not just between people but also between the realms, therefore it is good for meditative practices and also for help with study and learning. The colour is also used to symbolize water.

GREEN This colour, which belongs to Venus, promotes love, fertility, beauty, prosperity and wealth. Associated with the Earth in its guise of the Green Man and with the Great Mother in her nurturing form, it suggests emotional healing and growth.

GOLD AND YELLOW represent vitality, strength and rejuvenation. They are therefore used to promote physical healing, hope and happiness. Related to the Sun Gods and the element of air, they may also be used for protection.

ORANGE Used as a healing vibration, particularly of relationships, orange is also associated with material success and legal matters. A highly creative vibration, it often relates to childhood and emotional stability.

RED is recognized as being associated with passion, sexual potency and intensity. It is also representative of fire, with the qualities of courage and the healing of the blood and heart.

PINK signifies friendship, love, fidelity and the healing of emotions. It also symbolizes creativity and innocence, and is associated with the Goddess in her aspect of Maiden.

BROWN promotes the healing of the Earth, symbolizes the hearth and home, and is connected with the animal kingdom. It can also be used for the blending of several intentions.

BLACK is not a colour but rather the absence of both light and colour. It can therefore be used to banish negativity. It is often seen as the colour of the Goddess in her Wise Woman form.

Make each spell your own

For each of the spells in this book, we give a list of ingredients and special articles that may be required to achieve a result for that particular working. Because every individual spell maker brings their own energy into the process, you may find that you intuitively want to change something, whether that is an ingredient, a container or the words used. That is absolutely fine, and means that your spell has a very personal feel to it.

Above all, try to notice how your thoughts are driving your emotions and behaviour, and be aware of the sights, sounds, smells and tastes of the present moment as you go through the steps of each spell. Doing this will help you to experience things afresh and in a mindful way, and will help you to break free from the past and future.

HEALTH
and
HEALING

What goes on in the body is heavily influenced by what goes on in the mind, and mindfulness can be an enormously positive factor in promoting wellbeing – as the mind changes, so too does the body. Any form of holistic healing necessarily involves a combination of physical, emotional and spiritual changes, and this chapter features mindful spells that can help with the mental aspects of health and healing, including dispersing negative emotion, healing a depression, improving your sleep and healing others.

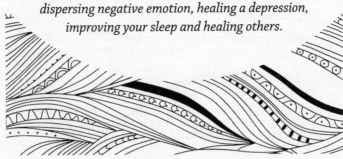

Good health wishing spell

This spell is worked at the time of the New Moon and is incredibly simple to do. Bay leaves possess a great deal of magical power and are used for granting wishes. This spell can be used to fulfil a range of desires, and is used here to bring about health and happiness.

 YOU WILL NEED
- ✦ 3 BAY LEAVES
- ☽ PIECE OF PAPER
- ● PENCIL OR PEN

 METHOD

During a New Moon, write your wish on a piece of paper and visualize it coming true.

Fold the paper into thirds, placing the three bay leaves inside.

Fold the paper towards you.

Again, visualize your wish coming true.

Fold the paper into thirds a second time, thus forming an envelope.

Keep it hidden in a dark place.

Reinforce your wish by repeatedly visualizing it coming true.

When the wish comes true, burn the paper as a mark of thanks.

● This little envelope of power can also be included in a mojo or talisman bag to add more power to it. In that case, try to be as specific as you can in your wish. You can impose a time limit on the spell coming to fruition, although it is often better not to do so.

 *Healing the body*

This spell works on a simple principle, that of identifying within the body whether the pain it is suffering is physical, emotional or, as is often the case, has a more deep-rooted spiritual component. It uses visualization and colour as its vehicles, and calls on Raphael the Archangel of Healing for help.

 YOU WILL NEED
✦ LARGE PIECE OF PAPER
➴ RED, YELLOW AND PURPLE FELT TIP PENS
● BLACK MARKER PEN

 METHOD

Draw three concentric circles.

The inner one should be purple, the middle yellow and the outer red.

Add a circle for the head and lines for the legs, so you have drawn a representation of yourself.

Now, thinking of any health difficulties you have, use the black marker to put a small mark on the drawn 'body' to represent that pain.

Keep your pen in contact with the paper and ask Raphael for help.

You might say:

 Raphael, Raphael Angel of ease,

Help me to understand this pain, please.

You should find that your mark is closer to one circle than the other.

Remembering that this method is not a self-diagnostic tool at all – it is simply designed to help you to come to terms with the pain or difficulty – note which colour this is:

- ✦ Red represents pain that is purely physical.
- ☽ Yellow usually signifies an emotional cause.
- ● Purple tends to have a more spiritual basis.

Sit quietly and draw that colour into yourself as though you were marking within your body where the pain is.

Next, mentally flood that part of your body with white light.

For the next two days, sit quietly and make the invocation to Raphael again.

Repeat the drawing-in of colour and the flooding with white light. At the end of that time you should begin to have an understanding of the causes of your pain and how your body is reacting to trauma.

● It must be stressed that this method is not designed as a substitute for medical diagnosis. It is a method of pain management which links with subtle energies to bring about healing on different levels. You may need to explore further some of the insights this gives you.

Healing may not be so much about getting better, as about letting go of everything that isn't you — all of the expectations, all of the beliefs — and becoming who you are.

Rachel Naomi Remen

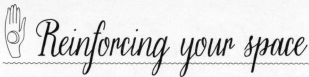# Reinforcing your space

This spell is representational. It uses a mirror to represent
light and power, and also employs numerology (the power
of numbers) in the nine white candles.

YOU WILL NEED
- ✦ MIRROR
- ☽ 9 WHITE CANDLES
- ● PROTECTION INCENSE
- ◗ EASILY HELD ROUND MIRROR
- ⚡ REPRESENTATION OF THE GODDESS

METHOD

Light the incense.

Place the candles in a ring around the Goddess image.

Light the candles, beginning with the candle most directly
before the Goddess image, and each time repeat these or
similar words:

 Light of Luna, protect me now.

When all are lit, hold the mirror so that it reflects the light
of the candles.

Turn slowly in each direction, ensuring that you throw the
light as far as you can in each direction.

Then spin around as many times as you have candles,
continuing to project the light and say:

 Goddess of love, goddess of light, protect this space.

Pinch out the candles and put them away safely.

● This technique is slightly unusual in that you pinch out
the candles rather than allowing them to burn down. This
is because it is the intensity of light that is required, not
the length of time it burns.

Glamour spell

In many ways this is a spell about loving yourself, hence the use of pink candles and love oil. In the use of incantation you are making a link with the principle of beauty and the Goddess of Beauty in one of her forms.

 YOU WILL NEED
- ✦ AT LEAST ONE PINK CANDLE, OR MORE IF YOU PREFER
- ☽ HANDHELD MIRROR
- ● LOVE OIL

METHOD

Dress the candle(s) with the love oil, working towards you since you want to feel differently about yourself.

Have in mind your ideal qualities of beauty as you do so.

Light the candles and stare deeply into the mirror.

See first the person you are now.

Visualize the change you want.

Then 'see' the person you would like to be.

Recite the following incantation out loud:

 Sacred flame as you dance

Call upon my sacred glance.

Call upon my better self,

Give me [your request].

Blessed flame shining brightly,

Bring about the changes nightly.

Give me now my second chance,

My beauty and glamour please enhance.

Power of three, let them see, let them see, let them see.

You can now snuff out the candle and relight it the next night, burning it for at least an hour.

Repeat the incantation at least three times.

● The power of visualization is a very strong tool. Each of us has an inner beauty which, if we work with it, is a tremendous help in daily life. Once we are prepared to recognize inner beauty in ourselves, it becomes evident to other people. This spell accomplishes that recognition.

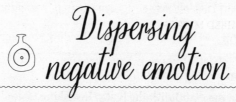

Dispersing negative emotion

Here is a simple technique for dealing with negative energies such as anger and resentment. It uses the elements and their qualities in a very positive way. The circle of light links with spirit, the dark stone represents earth, and the water acts in its cleansing capacity.

 YOU WILL NEED
✦ A DARK STONE

 METHOD

Visualize a circle of light around yourself.

Hold the dark stone in your hands.

Place it over your solar plexus.

Allow the negative emotion, perhaps anger and resentment, to flow into the stone.

Try to decide what colour the emotion is, and how it arose in the first place.

It sometimes helps to counteract such an emotion by changing its colour.

Raise the stone first to your forehead to signify clarity. Then place it over your heart (this helps to raise the healing vibration to the correct level).

If it seems right, use words such as:

 With this stone

Negative be gone,

Let water cleanse it

Back where it belongs.

This reinforces the idea of the stone holding your anger.

Concentrate and project all your negative emotion (anger, resentment etc) into the stone.

Visualize the emotion being sealed inside the stone.

Now with all your energy, take the stone to a source of running water in the open air.

It also helps if you can get up to a high place to throw your stone away, since this way you are using air as well as water.

• This spell uses the elements to clear away negative emotion, leaving space for positivity and good new things to come into your life. Under no circumstances should you allow the anger and resentment to build up again.

Moon power

This spell can be performed indoors as well as outside. It is representational since you use a paper moon or flower. In the incantation, the Moon is represented as a white swan. This should be done at the time of the Full Moon, and is designed to bring the energy of the Moon within your grasp until the next Full Moon.

 YOU WILL NEED
- ✦ BOWL OF WATER
- ☽ WHITE PAPER MOON OR FLOWER

 METHOD

Float the paper moon or flower in the bowl.

Raise the bowl towards the Moon in the sky and say:

Hail to thee white swan on the river.

Present life, tide turner,

Moving through the streams of life, all hail.

Mother of old and new days,

To you, through you, this night we cling to your aura.

Pure reflection, total in belief, touched by your presence,

I am in your power and wisdom.

Praise your power, your peace, my power, my peace.

I am strong. I praise. I bless.

Replace the bowl on your altar. Stand for a few moments, appreciating the power of the Moon.

• This spell is purely an incantation to the Moon and is therefore very simple. It needs no other tools or techniques except a physical representation of the Moon. Water is sacred to the Moon, and therefore we offer her that which belongs to her.

Overcoming
your shadows

This spell, which signifies letting go of the hurts of the past in a way that allows you to move forward with fresh energy into the future, can be performed at the time of the New Moon. By carrying it out every New Moon, you are gradually able to cleanse yourself of the detritus of the past, often as far back as childhood.

YOU WILL NEED
- ✦ CEDAR OR SAGE SMUDGING STICK, OR CLEANSING INCENSE
- ☽ WHITE CANDLE
- ● ATHAME OR RITUAL KNIFE
- ◖ BELL
- ⚡ CAKES AND WINE OR JUICE

METHOD

Cast your circle using the smudge stick or incense to 'sweep' the space as you move around the circle clockwise.

Think of your space as being dome-shaped over your head, and cleanse that space too.

Ring the bell.

With your arms raised, palms facing upwards, acknowledge the Goddess and say:

Great Goddess,

Queen of the Underworld,

Protector of all believers in you,

It is my will on this night of the New Moon

To overcome my shadows and bring about change.

I invite you to this my circle to assist and protect me in my rite.

Hold your athame or knife in your hands in acknowledgement of the God and say:

 Great God,

Lord of the Upper realms,

Friend of all who work with you,

It is my will on this night of the New Moon

To overcome my shadows and bring about change.

I invite you to my circle to assist me and protect me in my rite.

Light the candle and say:

 Behind me the darkness, in front of me the light,

As the wheel turns, I know that every end is a beginning.

I see birth, death and regeneration.

Spend a little time in quiet thought. If you can remember a time either in the last month or previously when times have not been good for you, concentrate on that.

While the candle begins to burn properly, remember what that time felt like.

Now concentrate on the candle flame and allow yourself to feel the positivity of the light.

Pick up the candle and hold it high above your head.

Feel the energy of the light shower down around you, and the negativity drain away.

Next, draw the power of the light into you and feel the energy in every pore.

Pass the candle around you and visualize the energy building up.

If you wish, say:

 Let the light cast out darkness.

Now ground yourself by partaking of the food and drink.

Thank the God and Goddess for their presence.

Withdraw from the circle.

• This is a very personal way for you to acknowledge the God and Goddess in your everyday life. While on first acquaintance it appears to be a protection technique, it is actually one to enhance your energies and to allow you to be healthy and happy in all levels of existence.

 # Healing a depression

Depression is not an easy illness to handle, and you should never regard spells such as this as a substitute for professional medical care. However, a mojo or talisman bag can be of tremendous support in the process of getting better, and has the effect of continually 'topping up' the energy needed to overcome difficulty.

YOU WILL NEED
- ✦ RED FLANNEL POUCH OR TALISMAN BAG
- ☽ PIECE OF ANGELICA ROOT FOR A WOMAN, OR PINE CONE FOR A MAN
- ● SPRIG OF ROSEMARY
- ◖ SMALL DOG TAG, LUCKY COIN OR TOKEN
- ⚡ WHITE CANDLE
- ◗ CLARY SAGE OIL TO DRESS THE OBJECTS AND TO USE AS INCENSE
- ◖ YOUR BURIN OR A PIN

METHOD

If the person you are helping is a woman, inscribe her initial on the angelica root and dress it with some of the clary sage oil.

If you are helping a man, do the same but use the pine cone instead.

When using a lucky token or charm, take care to dedicate it specifically to the person concerned.

Say something like:

 May this token of good luck bring healing to [name of person].

Inscribe the dog tag, lucky coin or token either with the person's initials, their astrological sign or the rune symbol Kenaz for inner strength, which is:

Repeat the words above as you do this.

Now place the objects in the pouch.

Light your candle and the incense.

Dress the bag itself by dropping a little oil on it.

Pass the bag and its contents through the incense smoke, all the while visualizing your subject as being well and happy.

Pass it over the candle three times, asking your favourite deity to help you in your task.

Give the bag to the person concerned, asking them to keep it with them at all times for at least a week.

● Your subject should sense an improvement in mood within the week. You can reinforce the bag's efficiency every now and again by burning a candle for a short while and directing the energy at the bag. If you are not able to give the bag to the person concerned, then hang it somewhere prominent so that you are reminded of them occasionally and can send loving energy their way.

Healing image spell

This spell uses the very old technique of representing a person as a poppet or small doll. It is similar to 'To know the child within' (pages 69–70), except that the poppet represents another person. Remember that healing takes place in the way that the recipient needs, not necessarily in the way we think it should happen.

 YOU WILL NEED
- ✦ POPPET
- ☽ BLUE CANDLE
- ● SALT WATER

 METHOD

Following the instructions on pages 29–30, create your poppet to represent the person you wish to help already completely healed and whole.

Take the doll into your sacred space.

Light the blue candle (to represent healing).

Sprinkle your poppet with the salt water.

Say:

This figure I hold made by my art

Here represents [name person],

By my art made, by my art changed,

Now may he/she be healed,

By art divine.

Pass the poppet quickly through the flame of the candle and visualize the person being cleansed of their problem.

Hold the poppet in both hands, breathe gently on it and visualize first the poppet and then the person being filled with divine healing energy.

Pay particular attention to the areas in the physical body of your friend with which you know they are having difficulty.

Imbue the poppet with the idea of being healed from a mental perspective.

Think of spiritual energy infusing the doll, and therefore your friend, with the spiritual help that they need.

Visualize the person concerned being completely filled with white light, well, happy and filled with energy.

Keep the poppet in your sacred space until it is no longer needed.

At this time, enter your sacred space, take the poppet, sprinkle it with water and say:

 By divine art changed,

By my art made,

Free this poppet from the connection with [name].

Let it now be unmade.

If the poppet contains direct links with the person – such as hair – burn it in an open fire. If it does not contain direct links, dispose of it in any way you wish.

If you have used a crystal at any point in this spell, this should be cleansed by holding it under running water, and perhaps then give it to the person as a keepsake or for protection.

• In this spell you are not just asking for alleviation of the symptoms; you are asking for help from a holistic perspective. Whenever you are working on someone else's behalf, you have a responsibility not to do anything that will make matters worse for them, therefore think very seriously before using this method.

Mindfulness is about being fully awake in our lives. It is about perceiving the exquisite vividness of each moment. We also gain immediate access to our own powerful inner resources for insight, transformation, and healing.

Jon Kabat-Zinn

Healing others

This is a spell using crystals, candles and incense. It is also representational in that you use the paper to represent the person you are healing.

 YOU WILL NEED
- ✦ 3 CANDLES: BLUE FOR HEALING, WHITE FOR POWER AND PINK FOR LOVE
- ☽ HEALING INCENSE (1 PART ALLSPICE, 1 PART ROSEMARY)
- ● PAPER WITH NAME OF THE PERSON YOU WISH TO BE HEALED
- ◗ CLEAR QUARTZ CRYSTAL

METHOD

Place the candles on the altar or in your sacred space in a semicircle, with the white candle in the middle.

Allow the incense to be on the left if the recipient is a woman; on the right if male. Light the incense.

Place the paper with the person's name in the centre.

Put the quartz crystal on top of the paper.

Be aware of your own energy linking with whatever you consider to be the Divine.

Breathe in the incense and feel your energy increasing.

When you feel ready, release the energy.

Imagine it passing through the crystal – which enhances it – to the recipient.

As you are doing this, say:

 [Name] be healed by the gift of this Power.

- A physical condition may not necessarily be healed, but you may have started an overall healing process. Often the person is given the emotional strength to withstand their trials and tribulations so that an inner healing occurs.

# Magical writing

This spell uses magically charged paper and ink. If your request is to increase something, it should be done between the New Moon and the Full Moon. To minimize or get rid of something, then it should be done during the Dark of the Moon or when the Moon is on the wane.

 YOU WILL NEED

- ✦ PAPER (EITHER REAL PARCHMENT OR PARCHMENT TYPE)
- ☽ QUILL PEN OR, IF YOU CAN FIND ONE, A FEATHER SHARPENED TO A POINT
- ● INK IN THE CORRECT COLOUR FOR YOUR REQUEST (SEE PAGES 35–6)
- ◖ CANDLE, AGAIN IN THE CORRECT COLOUR FOR YOUR REQUEST
- ⚡ APPROPRIATE INCENSE

 METHOD

Light the candle and the incense (for instance, use green for fertility or money, and perhaps blue for healing).

Write out your request carefully.

Some people may write it three times, others nine. Simply do what feels right for you.

Hold the paper in the smoke from the incense for as long as feels right.

Fold the paper into three and place it under the candle.

Let the candle burn out, but just before it does, burn the paper in the flame.

Alternatively, you might bury the paper in fresh earth and allow time to work slowly. As you become more proficient, use your intuition to guide you.

● This spell relies on a principle similar to that of sending a letter to Santa Claus. The magically charged paper can also be used to address the gods by name, and can be used for yourself and on behalf of others. If you petition for others, however, do not tell them what you are doing, as this nullifies the good. Using magically charged paper and ink can become an integral part of your spell making.

You may like to have some paper ready prepared and charged so that as your knowledge of symbolism increases, rather than writing out your request in longhand, you can use symbols to signify your desires. You might, for instance, use a key to symbolize your need for a house, a picture of an anvil to suggest partnership, and a sheaf of corn to suggest abundance. You could also use symbolic languages such as the runes.

 # Physical body change

In this spell you are using the power of the crystal to make changes. By bringing the problem out into the open, you are creating a way to a change on an inner level, instigating healing with it. This can be done at the time of the New Moon.

 YOU WILL NEED
- ✦ SMALL PIECE OF PAPER
- ☽ PEN
- ● QUARTZ CRYSTAL
- ◗ SOME STRING

METHOD

Take the piece of paper and write your name on it.

Draw on it what part of the body you want changed and what you want to look like.

If you want to change more than one area, draw the whole body and mark what you would like to change.

Hold the paper in your hands and imagine the body part changing from what it looks like now to what you want it to look like.

Fold the paper up any way you like and tie it to the crystal.

Once more, visualize the body part changing again.

When you feel that changes are taking place, untie the string, tear the paper up and scatter it to the wind.

If you wish, you can bury the crystal to signify the fact that you have internalized the changes you have made.

● This spell is very good for changing aspects you don't like. It may take a few days or even longer to see results, so you need to be patient. The spell should not be used to try to heal any conditions of a medical nature.

 # Purifying emotions

This spell will help you to release the negativity and distress that may build up when you do not feel that you are in control of your life. It uses the four elements to do this, and may be performed on any evening during a Waning Moon. It has been kept deliberately simple so that you can spend more time in learning how to make your emotions work for you rather than letting them overwhelm you.

 YOU WILL NEED
- ✦ WHITE CANDLE
- ☽ BOWL OF WATER
- ● BOWL OF SALT
- ◐ DRIED HERBS (SUCH AS SAGE FOR WISDOM)
- ⚡ VESSEL IN WHICH THE HERBS CAN BE BURNED

 METHOD
Stand in your sacred space and say:

I call upon the elements in this simple ceremony that I may be cleansed from the contamination of negativity.

Wave your hand over or through the flame and say:

🪶 🪶 *I willingly release negative action in my fire.*

Rub salt on your hands and say:

🪶 🪶 *I release stumbling blocks and obstacles in my earth.*

Light the herbs, wave the smoke in front of you, inhale the perfume as it burns and say:

🪶 🪶 *I clear my air of unwise thoughts.*

Dip your hands in the water and say:

🪶 🪶 *I purify this water.*

   Let this relinquishing be gentle.

   Purified, cleansed and released in all ways,

   I now acknowledge my trust and faith in my own clarity.

Spend a little time thinking about the next few weeks to come.

Recognize that there may be times when you need the clarity you have just requested.

Now dispose of the ingredients immediately.

Put the salt in with the ashes, then pour the water on the ground so that it mingles with the ashes and salt.

● It is helpful to find some sort of ceremonial way of releasing energy, enabling you to let go of an old situation. A good time to do this is just before a New Moon, so that you can begin a fresh cycle with renewed vigour.

To cure sickness

Knot magic is good for getting rid of illnesses, and this spell will help to do this. It works on the principle of binding an illness into a cord, so it is a form of sympathetic magic combined with positive thought.

 YOU WILL NEED
- ✦ LENGTH OF CORD, ABOUT 8 IN (20 CM) LONG
- ☽ PENCIL AND PAPER
- ● CONTAINER OF SALT

METHOD

Mark the cord six times so that you have seven equal lengths.

Take a few deep breaths and feel your energy connecting with the Earth.

Repeat the following words six times, and tie a knot in the cord each time:

 Sickness, no one bids you stay.

It's time for you to fade away.

Through these knots I bid you leave,

By these words which I do weave.

Put the cord in the container of salt (this represents burying in the earth).

Create a seal for the container with the above incantation written on the paper.

Dispose of the container, perhaps in running water.

● The number six has particular relevance here: it is widely accepted as the number of the Sun, which is restorative and regenerative.

Petition to the Horned God

Cernunnos means 'The Horned One', and in this spell he is invoked as the God of hidden knowledge and of movement through our own difficulties. Because of his virility, he has a lust for life that we all need. The spell is probably best done at sunrise and in the open air.

YOU WILL NEED

- ✦ A CLEAR SPACE IN WOODS
- ☽ STONE MARKERS FOR THE FOUR COMPASS DIRECTIONS
- ● SOME GREEN BRANCHES (PREFERABLY OAK, BUT OTHERWISE YOUR FAVOURED SACRED TREE)

METHOD

Place your stones according to the four directions, and listen to the sounds around you while you do this.

You may become aware of a change in energy, in which case acknowledge the presence of the nature spirits.

Place the branches (sacred to Cernunnos) close to the centre where you are working, which has now become your sacred space.

Stand in the centre of your sacred space.

Put your hands in the God position (arms outstretched).

Say:

 Great Horned Leader of the Hounds

Lord Cernunnos hear my call

You, who move with the rhythm of the forests

Upon your knowledge let me draw

Potent Huntsman who dances with the serpent

Of knowledge, forever virile and gracious

Grant me the power of potent movement

Let me move too within the mysterious

Speaker with the ancient shamans

Who bridge this world and the next

Unstoppable as force of nature

Aid my footsteps forward free from the past.

Stand still, quietly drawing on the power of Cernunnos as you contemplate your next move in life.

Deliberately put the past behind you and resolve to move forward with courage and speed.

When your ceremony is complete, scatter the stones and branches so that you leave no trace behind.

• This is not a spell to help you make a decision, but more one to increase your energy levels. It will help you to move forward swiftly and allow matters to drop into place so that your path forward can be unimpeded. The assumption is that you have already decided what you want to do.

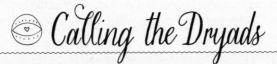

Calling the Dryads

As you become more proficient at using energies, you will find a need to link with nature spirits and spirits of the elements. These energies are very subtle, and the incantations used in this spell acknowledge that subtlety.

 YOU WILL NEED
- ✦ BIRTHDAY CANDLES IN DIFFERENT COLOURS
- ☽ HALF NUTSHELLS SUCH AS WALNUTS, OR ICE CREAM STICKS
- ● WATER IN A NATURAL POOL, POND OR BOWL

METHOD

Use different-coloured candles to attract different 'families' of Dryad.

Fix the candles into the half shells or onto the slivers of wood using hot wax from a burning candle. (This can be very fiddly; use half candles if this is easier.)

Light each candle with a blessing and float your 'boats' on the surface of the water.

Send loving thoughts to the nature spirits and ask them to join you.

You might use an invocation such as:

Awake you spirits of the forest green

Join me now

Let yourselves be seen.

Now sit quietly and just listen.

Shortly you will sense the presence of the Dryads, often when you hear strange rustlings in the trees or vegetation.

You may feel them as they brush past you or play around you. Initially you will probably not be able to differentiate between them, but as time goes on you will sense subtle differences.

Half close your eyes and see if you can see them. Again, don't be too disappointed if nothing happens immediately. Just accept that you will be aware of them eventually.

Now, invite them to play with you:

Come, Dryads all, come join with me

Explore Earth, Sky, Sand and Sea

Show me, guide me, take my hands

Together thus, we see new lands

New vistas, new horizons and knowledge of old

Come together, in power enfold.

When they are comfortable with you, and you with them, thank the Dryads for coming, then leave the area tidy.

You can leave the candles to burn out if it is safe to do so.

• While it may seem strange to be invoking spirits of earth or greenery, a little thought will show you that all living things are interconnected, and this is simply one way of making such a connection.

The spell of the shell

This is a lunar spell calling on the power of the Moon and the waves. It is also representational because the shell is a long-accepted symbol for the Goddess and signifies her ability to take all things to her and effect changes. In this example, we use an Ogham Stave to represent healing, although the spell can be used for other purposes as well.

 YOU WILL NEED
- ✦ A SHELL
- ☽ SYMBOL OF YOUR DESIRE
- ● FINE-NIBBED MARKER PEN

METHOD

To perform this spell, you must first find a suitable shell in shallow water.

Take the shell and dry it thoroughly.

Draw your chosen symbol upon the surface of the shell.

For healing, we suggest the Edhadh Ogham Stave:

Place the shell on the shore, so that the tide will bring the waves across it.

When the shell is in place, draw a triangle in the sand, enclosing the shell completely.

The symbol upon the shell must be facing upwards (towards the Moon).

Meaningful words or phrases may also be placed upon the shell, or simply written in the sand (inside the triangle).

Finally, face the Moon and say the following words of enchantment:

 Goddess of Moon, Earth and Sea,

Each wish in thy name must come to be.

Powers and forces which tides do make,

Now summon thy waves, my spell to take.

Leave the area now, and the spell is set.

Once the waves come, your wish will be taken out to the spirits of the sea.

It will usually take about seven days for a lunar spell to begin to manifest, but it can take as long as 28 days.

• This type of magic is what we called 'little works', and belongs to the folk-magic level of spell making. Take care to note the phases of the Moon (waxing for the gain of something; waning for the dissolving of something). You are using natural objects that seemingly mean nothing to the uninitiated.

To clear evil intent

**This spell can be used if you suspect that somebody is
directing unhelpful energy towards you, making you
sick. Words have particular force, so in expressing your
feelings forcibly (as in line 2 of the incantation), you are
turning the energy back on the perpetrator.**

 YOU WILL NEED
- ✦ LENGTH OF STRING
- ☽ BOTTLE

 METHOD

Tie a knot in the string.

Place it in the bottle and bury it in the earth.

After three days, dig it up.

Put the bottle on the floor or ground and say:

> *A curse on me you buried deep*
>
> *To make me sick, you nasty creep.*
>
> *I placed a knot into this twine*
>
> *And so your work was worked in vain.*

Shatter the bottle, carefully pick up the string and undo
the knot; the original curse is now invalid.

Dispose of the bottle remains in any way that you feel
is appropriate.

Burn the cord and blow the ashes to the wind.

● In some ways, this could be called a protection spell,
but since the 'curse' could cause you to be ill, the spell
guards your wellbeing. The curse is transferred by the
power of your spell to the cord, which is then disposed of
by burning. The assumption is that your magic is stronger
than the person who has wished you ill.

We do so much, we run so quickly, the situation is difficult, and many people say, "Don't just sit there, do something." But doing more things may make the situation worse. So you should say, "Don't just do something, sit there." Sit there, stop, be yourself first, and begin from there.

Thich Nhat Hanh

To drive away bad dreams

Herbal magic and correspondences are used in this spell to clear your bedroom of negative influences. It is always a good idea to use material that is easily available, so you might like to use sprigs of rosemary, sage, lady's bedstraw or maize silks (broom corn). Since you want something taken away, you should perform this magical spell as the Moon wanes.

YOU WILL NEED
* BOWL OF WARM WATER
* SALT
* SPRIGS OF HERBS
* STRING

METHOD

Dissolve the salt in the warm water.

Tie the herbs together.

Dip the sprigs in the water and sprinkle the corners of the room with the water.

Next, use the sprigs to sprinkle the salt water on your bedclothes, and particularly around the head and foot of your bed.

When you have done this, place the herbs under your pillow, or if you prefer, under the middle of the bed.

The next morning, discard the herbs at a crossroads if you can, either by burying them or allowing them to disperse to the four winds.

Otherwise, ensure that you have carried them well away from your home.

This carries all negativity away from your bedroom and bed.

• This spell uses rosemary which brings clarity, sage for wisdom, lady's bedstraw which is said to have lined the manger at Christ's birth, and maize silks or broom corn which is used in worship of the Mexican goddess Chicomecoatl. All of these bring cleansing, not just of the room but also of the occupant's aura or subtle energy.

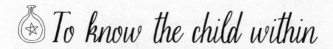 To know the child within

This spell is a variation on a technique which appreciates that we all have aspects of ourselves that can go unrecognized and therefore undeveloped. By using your sacred space in which to work, you are enhancing the connection you make to that part of you that remains childlike. The main tool is visualization.

 YOU WILL NEED
- ✦ GREEN OR BLUE CANDLE, TO SIGNIFY HEALING
- ☽ INCENSE OR ESSENTIAL OIL THAT REMINDS YOU OF YOUR CHILDHOOD
- ● DOLL OR POPPET, TO SIGNIFY THE CHILD YOU ONCE WERE
- ◐ SALT WATER
- ⚡ WHITE CLOTH
- ◗ YOUR ALTAR, WHICH COULD JUST BE A TABLE THAT YOU DEDICATE TO THE PURPOSE

 METHOD

Light your candle and the incense.

Choose a particularly good childhood memory.

Hold the poppet in your arms and think about the child you once were.

Now treat the poppet as though it were a child. Say:

 I name you [use your own childhood name or nickname].

Hold the poppet in your arms, croon to it, rock it, and talk to it. Tell it everything you would have liked to hear as a child.

Imagine that it talks to you and tells you how it feels and what it wants. You may even hear your own childish voice.

Let your own voice change in response. Play with the poppet.

Now become aware of your adult self again.

Sprinkle the doll with a little salt water to cleanse away the negative past.

Raise your own energy by whatever method you prefer – breathing, colour, a brief meditation or an appeal to the gods.

Visualize yourself pouring that positive energy into the doll, which represents your own inner self.

Imagine the child you would've liked to have been, and project that image into your doll.

Continue until you can feel a change in the energy and you feel at peace.

(During this time you may find that you are crying or laughing just like a child. This is simply a release of energy, and is perfectly acceptable.)

You may find that the poppet or doll begins to feel vibrant and alive, glowing with white light and love.

Kiss the doll.

Wrap it in white cloth as you would a baby, and lay it to rest on your altar.

Leave the candle to burn out.

Leave your sacred space secure.

• It is important that you give yourself time afterwards to return to normal, so you need to spend a little time just appreciating the person you have become. Ground yourself by whatever method you choose – touching the ground, taking a walk, having a bath, or whatever you prefer.

A nurturing activity such as cooking is also good. You will probably find after this technique that you tend to dream somewhat vividly, as you uncover some of the joys and hurts of childhood.

Attaining radiant health

This spell uses invocation to enable you to attain and maintain radiant and perpetual health. You can enhance the energy by finding an open space, free of pollution, and using sunlight, moonlight, wind or rain as part of the process. Sunday is an ideal day to perform the spell, as this is the day that health matters are highlighted.

YOU WILL NEED
- ✦ AN OPEN SPACE OR YOUR SACRED SPACE
- ☽ YOUR OWN BODY
- ● CORIANDER SEEDS TIED IN A SMALL MUSLIN BAG

METHOD

First sense your own aura – your subtle energies which make you unique.

Hold your hands over your heart area, then move them down to just below your solar plexus. You should sense a change in energy in your hands.

This is the point in your body sometimes called the 'point of power', the place where your life energy resides.

Now, facing east with your arms spread wide and the palms of your hands upwards, say the following:

Great God of the Heavens, and Lord of all Power,

Grant me the right to feel and perceive the true life force that is mine,

So that I may have everlasting wellbeing.

Grant me, O Great God, this favour.

Now run your hands around your body from top to toe in a sweeping motion, not quite touching your body.

Raise your arms again and visualize a universal healing energy sweeping towards you as you repeat the incantation.

Take a deep breath, visualizing and feeling the energy being drawn in and down to the solar plexus.

As you slowly exhale, see the energy travelling to your extremities and filling you with power and healing.

Do this at least three times or for up to 15 minutes at a time.

Place your hands on your point of power and repeat the incantation a third time, this time sensing the energy settling into your point of power.

If you are in an open space, become aware of the power of sunlight, moonlight, wind or rain.

Finally, take a ritual bath into which you have put the coriander seeds.

● The purpose of this spell is not to cure you of any specific ailment, but to help your overall health by enhancing your energy. Please always seek the services of a qualified doctor or health practitioner if you know or suspect that your health is compromised in any way.

To enhance confidence

In the olden days many people thought that noise was a way of getting rid of demons, so it was customary to shout when banishing such nasty things. Today we also recognize that psychologically we can be encouraged by passion, so this is a method of self-encouragement and an appeal to our own inner demons.

YOU WILL NEED
- ✦ BELL OR RATTLE
- ♪ ROUSING MUSIC
- ● YOUR VOICE

METHOD

Choose a short affirmation that expresses your best hopes for yourself.

These might be:

 I will survive.

I can overcome any problem.

I have the confidence to do anything.

I am my own best friend.

Preferably choose a time when you will not disturb others, and when you will not be disturbed.

Play your music until you feel uplifted by its mood.

Take up your bell or rattle and dance around the room.

Proclaim your affirmation at the top of your voice at least three times, and preferably nine. When the music finishes, resolve to do three different things in the next week, to demonstrate your new-found confidence.

Each week reaffirm your confidence in the same way, changing the words as necessary.

- This spell does seem to have an almost immediate effect. Even if you feel silly at first, having confidence is often about losing your inhibitions, and this is one way that can help. As a support for this, so that you have a visual image, have fun drawing your own demon, even if it is only as a stick figure.

A light spell

This spell enables us to practise in the safety of our sacred space before venturing out into the everyday world. It is not so much a healing technique as an energizing one. The closer we come to an understanding of the powers that we use, the less we need protection and the more we can become a source of spiritual energy for others.

 YOU WILL NEED

- ✦ AS MANY WHITE CANDLES AS FEELS RIGHT (AN ODD NUMBER WORKS WELL)
- ☽ EQUIVALENT NUMBER OF HOLDERS
- ● ANOINTING OIL OF FRANKINCENSE

 METHOD

Anoint the candles from middle to bottom, then from middle to top. This is to achieve a balance of physical and spiritual energy.

Place the candles in the holders on the floor in a circle about 6 ft (1.8 m) in diameter.

Standing in the circle, light the candles in a clockwise direction.

Stand in the centre of the circle and 'draw' the energy of the light towards you.

Feel the energy as it seeps throughout the whole of your body, from your feet to your head.

Allow the energy to spill over from the crown of your head to fill the space around you.

It should feel like this around your body:

( )

Now, visualize this cocoon of light around you gently radiating outwards to the edge of your circle of candles.

When you feel ready, sit on the floor and allow the energy of the light to settle back within you.

Ground yourself by sweeping your body with your hands in the shape of the above figure, but do not lose the sense of increased energy.

Snuff out the candles in a clockwise direction, and use them only to repeat this technique until they are used up.

• Gradually, as you become used to the sense of increased energy, you should find that you are more able to cope with difficulties and be more dynamic in the everyday world. It will become easier to carry the light within you, not just within the circle of candles, and you may find that you perceive more ways in which you can 'help the world go around'.

 ## *A medication spell*

As you begin to understand colour correspondences, you can begin to use them in spells to keep you well. Many people have to take medication of one sort or another, and this spell helps to enhance the action of your particular one. You should take your medication at the times given by your health practitioner, but with this spell you can add additional potency.

YOU WILL NEED
- ✶ YOUR GIVEN MEDICATION
- ☽ HEALING INCENSE (MIXTURE OF ROSEMARY AND JUNIPER)
- ● ANOINTING OIL
- ◖ SQUARE OF PURPLE CLOTH
- ✦ WHITE CANDLE

METHOD

Anoint your candle with the oil.

Light your candle.

Light the incense and allow the smoke to surround you.

Sit quietly and imagine that you are well.

Really feel what it is like to be functioning fully.

Sense how the medication will help you.

Pick up your medication and allow the healing energy to flow through you to the medication.

When you feel it the medication is charged sufficiently, put it on the purple cloth and leave it there until the incense and the candle have burnt out.

Whenever you take your medication in the future, visualize the link between it and you, as it helps to alleviate whatever your problems are.

You can further help yourself before you take your prescription to the pharmacist by placing the prescription under a white candle and asking for it to be blessed.

• Do please remember that this technique is not a substitute for medication. You are asking for help in healing yourself and using everything that is available to you. The spell is designed to enhance the healing energy so that you can make maximum use of it. In working in this way, you will also be enabled to do all you can to make adjustments to your lifestyle and diet.

Cleansing the aura

This spell is a cleansing one that uses nothing but sound. It can be done anywhere, but in the open air is better. Whichever sound you use will depend on your own sense of yourself, but the one suggested here is known to be successful.

 YOU WILL NEED
* AN OPEN SPACE
* YOUR VOICE

METHOD

Find a spot in which you feel comfortable within your open space. The best spot will depend on what you are attempting to get rid of. Be sure to take plenty of time over choosing this, until it feels absolutely right.

Settle yourself comfortably on the ground.

Take a big deep breath and then breathe out.

Your breath out should be slightly longer than the in breath.

Do this three times to clear your lungs.

Now take a further deep breath. This time, as you exhale, say as loudly as you can:

 Ahh... Ee... Oo...

Repeat the sounds at least twice more, increasing in intensity each time until you are actually screaming.

If you can, continue for two more sets of three (nine times in all, although six is fine).

Sit quietly, place your hands on the earth or the floor, re-orientate yourself in your surroundings and absorb fresh energy as you do so.

Become aware of the sounds around you.

Leave the area.

● This is quite a powerful technique, and you need to be quiet for the rest of the day so that you can allow the energy to settle. This method is a good way of dealing with the frustrations of your everyday world, and often results in being able to look at things from a different perspective.

 *Fertility spell*

This spell employs symbolism in its use of a fig and an egg, and also features ancient methods of acknowledgement in the offering to Mother Earth for fertility. Crops were often offered to the goddess in the hope of a good harvest, and in this spell that hope is for new life. This technique is best done at the time of the New Moon, or alternatively in springtime when the Goddess of Fertility is commemorated.

 YOU WILL NEED
- ✦ FRANKINCENSE AND SANDALWOOD INCENSE
- ☽ WHITE CANDLE
- ● FIG (FRESH IF POSSIBLE)
- ◗ FRESH EGG
- ⚡ CLEAR GLASS BOWL
- ◢ MARKER PEN
- ◖ YOUR BOLINE
- ♥ TROWEL

 METHOD

Light your incense and the candle.

Put the egg on the left and the fig on the right, with the bowl in the middle.

Draw a symbol of your child on the egg.

Very carefully break the egg into the bowl, then replace the empty shell on the left side again.

Make a small cut in the fig with your boline, and carefully scrape the seeds into the bowl.

Place the remains of the fig into the eggshell to represent the physical baby within the womb, and again replace it on the left side.

With your finger, stir the contents of the bowl clockwise three times, and say:

 As these two become one

May the Goddess and the God

Bless our union with child.

Leave the bowl in the middle and allow the candle to burn out.

Take the bowl and the eggshell with its contents to a place where you can safely bury them.

Your own garden would be good if you have one, otherwise choose a quiet, secluded spot.

Place the eggshell in the ground and pour the contents of the bowl over it.

As you cover it with earth, say:

 I offer to Mother Earth

A symbol of fertility

In love and gratitude for her bounty.

Now await developments without feeling any anxiety.

• This spell is full of symbolism. The fig represents not only fertility, but is also thought to feed the psyche – that part of us some call the 'soul'. The egg is an ancient symbol of fertility, and indeed of the beginning of life. Bringing the two together acknowledges your sense of responsibility for the continuation of life.

Isis girdle

This spell is based on knot magic, and is used to ensure that your energy is at the right level for your magical work. Buckles, belts or girdles were often associated with Isis or Venus, and therefore aspects of femininity. They represent physical wellbeing and moral strength. This spell is ideally performed on a Wednesday.

 YOU WILL NEED

 ✦ 3 LENGTHS OF CORD, ABOUT 9 FT (3 M) EACH

METHOD

Before you begin, decide the purpose of your girdle.

To address health issues you might choose the colour blue, or to work from a spiritual perspective choose purple or white.

Begin braiding the cord, and as you do so, bear in mind that you are fashioning three aspects of self – body mind and spirit – to become one source of power in all that you do.

In this way, the braid becomes an extension of you and also a protector of your being.

Call on the power of Isis as you braid, to give you strength and determination.

Tie a knot in both ends to seal in the power.

Now consecrate the girdle by holding it in your non-dominant hand and circling it anti-clockwise three times with your dominant hand, saying words such as:

 Isis, Mistress of the Words of Power
Cleanse this girdle for my use.

See the girdle surrounded by light and glowing brightly.

Let the image fade.

Next, circle the girdle clockwise three times with your dominant hand, and say:

🪶 🪶 *Isis, Goddess of the Throne*
   Protect me from all ill.

Again, perceive the girdle surrounded by light.

Next, put the girdle around your waist and say:

🪶 🪶 *Isis, Goddess of Perceived Truth*
   Thy wisdom is reality.

This time, feel the energy in the girdle and say:

🪶 🪶 *I stand ready to do thy work.*

In future, each time you put on the girdle, you should be able to sense the energy, giving you the power to carry out your chosen task.

• This is quite a powerful spell to do. Not only does it protect you from illness, it also prepares you to be able to help others as they require it. Since Isis rules intuition, you will find that you are in a better position to understand others' pain and distress.

*You can't stop
the waves, but
you can learn
to surf.*

Jon Kabat-Zinn

Improving self-esteem

This spell uses candles, cord, colour and visualization, and requires very little effort – although it takes a week to finish. It is a spell that men can do very easily and will see and feel the tangible results. It works on self-esteem and virility.

 YOU WILL NEED
- ✦ 7 SHORT LENGTHS OF CORD, ABOUT 6 IN (15 CM) LONG
- ☽ 7 TEALIGHTS
- ● 7 SMALL SQUARES OF RED PAPER OR CLOTH

 METHOD

On returning from work, place a tealight on one red square.

Surround the tealight by the cord, laying it on the red square.

As you do so, say:

 This represents me and all I feel myself to be

I wish to be [strong, virile, at ease with myself – your choice of words].

Let the tealight burn out.

Next morning, knot both ends of the cord, saying as you do:

 This cord carries my intent to be [your choice of words].

Carry the cord with you, and when you need to, remind yourself during the day of your intent.

Repeat the procedure for seven nights using the same words and either the same intent or another that feels more appropriate.

Each morning, repeat the same procedure as the first morning.

At the end of the seven days, either tie the cords together in one loop (end to end) or tie them so they form a tassel.

Either way, hang them by your mirror where you cannot fail to see them.

Each morning for about six weeks choose which affirmation you wish to use that day, and make sure you have acted accordingly.

● This spell has a long-term effect on your personality. Each time you make the morning affirmation, you are calling on the power of the whole to assist you in being the sort of person you want to be. Any behaviour that does not fit that image soon drops away.

Sleep well

Smoky quartz is sometimes known as the 'dream stone'. It is an able tool for meditation, and helps you to explore your inner self by penetrating darker areas with light and love. Because of this, it is effective in releasing negativities such as grief, anger and despair by removing depression. It is mildly sedative and relaxing, and a good balancer of sexual energy. The cairngorm stone beloved of the Scots is a form of smoky quartz.

YOU WILL NEED
✦ PIECE OF SMOKY QUARTZ
☽ PIECE OF PAPER
● PEN
◗ YOUR BED

METHOD
When you have prepared your sleep environment, sit quietly while holding the smoky quartz, and bring to mind any old hurts, anger, depression and difficulties you may have.

Do not be afraid that doing this will bring on depression, because with this technique you are aiming to rid yourself of the depression that thoughts things bring.

Put aside the quartz for the moment and write down on the paper all that you have considered and thought about.

Now pass the quartz three times over the bed to absorb any negativity.

You might use the sign of infinity from top to bottom.

Wrap the paper around the quartz and place it under your pillow, with the intent that it will help you to overcome your pain and hurt.

Go to sleep, and in the morning remove the paper and dispose of it by tearing it up and flushing it away or burning it.

If you wish, you can repeat the process for the next two nights, by which time you should feel much relieved.

Finally, cleanse the stone under running water and keep it until you need it again, or dispose of it by going to a high place and throwing it away.

• Another use for smoky quartz is to reflect an intrusive energy back to the person concerned. If you are receiving unwanted attention from someone, place a piece of smoky quartz or cairngorm in your window and know that you can sleep protected.

A healing technique for someone else

There is a whole art in knot tying that arose among the Celtic people and later became an illustrative art. If you are able to do it, the reef knot – beloved of scouts and woodcrafters – is ideal for this spell, since it will not come undone. Tying a knot can also be used as healing for someone else.

YOU WILL NEED
★ LENGTH OF GRASS, STRING OR RIBBON

METHOD

This requires you to tie a double knot in your chosen material. In using material that will return to the earth and rot away, you must also think of the pain or difficulty as dissolving.

Tie one knot, going first from left to right, and saying words such as:

 Pain begone
'Tis now withdrawn.

Now tie a knot in the opposite direction, and use words such as:

 This pain is held
Its effects dispelled.

Now bury the knot, preferably well away from the person concerned.

As you bury it, give a blessing such as:

 Bless this place and make it pure
Ill gone for good we now ensure.

Now you can leave nature to do its work.

● In this spell you tie your knot with the idea of binding the pain and then getting rid of it. This may be a slow process if the condition is a long-standing one, and sometimes we have to remember that there are spiritual lessons to be learned through sickness. Obviously the person concerned should also have medical help, so part of your responsibility is to ensure that this happens. Do not feel that the spell has failed if changes are not seen; they may be taking place at a much deeper level.

Mars water

At one time, water charged with iron was considered to be a healing potion, creating a way of treating anaemia. Today it is considered to be more of a protective device and, when under attack, to enable you to send a curse or hex back where it belongs.

 YOU WILL NEED
✦ IRON NAILS OR FILINGS
☽ LARGE JAR WITH A LID
● ENOUGH WATER TO COVER THE NAILS OR FILINGS

 METHOD
Put the nails or filings in the jar and cover them with water.

Close the jar and leave undisturbed until rust begins to form.

The jar can be opened occasionally to check on its condition, which helps the formation of rust. This should take about seven to ten days.

After this time, the jar may be shaken and the water then strained and used as appropriate.

Keep adding water as necessary to the jar thereafter, to maintain its potency.

You should not need to renew the nails or filings unless the concoction begins to develop mould, in which case throw everything out and start again.

When using the water, you may like to give acknowledgement to Mars by using a form of words such as:

 Mars, God of War

Protect me now as I [state task].

● You can use some of the water in your ritual bath or to cleanse and empower your hands before an important event. A business situation that requires you to be more than usually aggressive might need a crystal charged in Mars water to make it especially powerful.

LOVE
and
RELATIONSHIPS

Building and maintaining positive bonds with other people is one of the most fulfilling things human beings can do, and it's important to be mindful of our feelings and what we are trying to achieve. Spells for improving love and relationships are not just about influencing someone else's feelings; they are equally about making us feel better about ourselves. This chapter features a range of spells that can help, such as creating opportunities for love, healing a rift, stopping an argument and easing a broken heart.

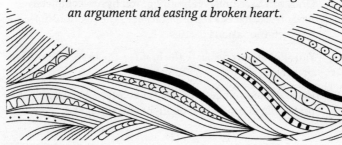

To clarify relationships

The art of braiding can be used in spell making to represent many things. In this particular spell, braiding is used to signify the coming together of three people, and in the unbraiding, an amicable resolution. In the use of colour, the spell is focused either on the outcome or on the people concerned.

YOU WILL NEED

* 3 LENGTHS OF RIBBON OF SUITABLE COLOUR – YOU CAN USE ASTROLOGICAL COLOURS TO REPRESENT EACH PERSON, OR YOU CAN USE ONE COLOUR TO REPRESENT THE SITUATION, FOR EXAMPLE:
  * RED FOR A RELATIONSHIP SOURED BY ANGER
  * BLUE FOR A BUSINESS RELATIONSHIP
  * GREEN FOR A RELATIONSHIP IN WHICH FINANCE IS IMPORTANT
  * YELLOW WHERE COMMUNICATION IS DIFFICULT

METHOD

Before you begin, decide what you are trying to achieve.

If it is important to bring people together, then you should concentrate on this as you are braiding.

If it is seen as necessary for people to go their separate ways, while you are braiding concentrate on the intricacies of the situation and perhaps the ability to bring about open and frank discussion.

Once you have finished braiding, you have a completely new object that is a representation of the relationship between the various parties.

You should now dedicate the braid to the best outcome for that relationship.

Put the braid somewhere safe for at least 72 hours, preferably in constant moonlight and sunlight.

Only when the reason for the relationship is fulfilled (e.g. reconciliation between people, full honest communication, or a successful business partnership) can you think of dismantling the braid.

As you undo the braid, ask that the people involved can go forward in life in whatever way is appropriate for them, gaining what they have needed from their association.

You may of course wish to keep the braid without undoing it.

Do not use the ribbons for any other magical purposes.

• A braiding spell is a type of knot spell, and is a gentle way of affecting the outcome of a situation. It is, of course, not necessarily a quick way of resolving anything, but is often surprising in its outcome.

 # *To focus your lover's interest*

If you find that your partner's attention seems to be wandering, try this spell. It is best performed on a Friday, the day sacred to Venus the Goddess of Love.

YOU WILL NEED
✦ CLEAN PIECE OF PAPER
☽ PEN THAT YOU LIKE

METHOD
Taking your pen, write your first name and your lover's surname on the paper.

Draw either a square or circle around them.

(Use the square if you decide that all you want is a physical relationship, and the circle if you are utterly convinced this person is right for you.)

With your eyes closed, say:

 If it be right, come back to me.

Cut the square or circle out and place it inside your pillowcase for at least three nights.

Your lover should show renewed interest.

● This is one spell that occasionally does not work. It is said that Venus will not assist if there is any intrinsic reason for the relationship not to work out. If your partner no longer loves you, for example, you may be unsuccessful in your aim. You must accept this, knowing that you have done the best you can.

To bring romantic love to you

This spell uses herbs, crystals, a candle and colour. The herb rosemary signifies long memory, the rose quartz crystal signifies love, and the colours signify love and passion. The method is designed to concentrate the mind and to attract love to you, as opposed to a specific lover.

YOU WILL NEED
- ✦ SPRIG OF ROSEMARY (FOR REMEMBRANCE)
- ☽ PIECE OF ROSE QUARTZ CRYSTAL
- ● ROSE OR VANILLA INCENSE
- ◐ PINK OR RED VOTIVE CANDLE
- ⚡ SMALL BOX
- ◗ RED MARKER OR PEN

METHOD
Sit in your own most powerful place. (That might be inside, outside, near your favourite tree or by running water.)

First, write in red on the box, 'Love is mine'.

Light the incense – this clears the atmosphere and puts you in the right mood.

Put the rosemary and the rose quartz in the box.

Put anything else that represents love to you in the box (drawings of hearts, poems, or whatever – be creative).

Remember, this spell is to attract love to you, not a specific lover, so don't use a representation of a particular person.

Be in a very positive state of mind.

Imagine yourself very happy and in love.

Burn the candle and say:

 I am love
Love I will find
True love preferably
Will soon be mine.

Love is me
Love I seek
My true love
I will soon meet.

Now sit for a little while and concentrate again on being happy.

Then pinch out the candle and add it to the box.

Let the incense burn out.

Seal the box shut and don't open it until you have found your true love.

When you have found your lover, take the rose quartz out of the box and keep it as a reminder.

Bury the entire box in the earth.

• Because you reproduce a positive state of mind and you are imagining what it is like to be in love in this spell, you set up a current of energy that attracts that feeling. In sealing the box, you 'capture' the vibration of love and all things become possible.

The most precious gift
we can offer others is
our presence. When
mindfulness embraces
those we love, they will
bloom like flowers.

Thich Nhat Hanh

To clear the air between lovers

When communication between you and your partner seems difficult, you can forge a new link using this spell, which is representational. You will need to have confidence in your own power, though.

YOU WILL NEED
- CRYSTAL BALL OR MAGNIFYING GLASS
- PHOTOGRAPH OF YOUR PARTNER

METHOD

Place the crystal ball or magnifying glass over the image of your partner's face.

Because the features are magnified, the eyes and mouth will appear to move and come to life.

Simply state your wishes or difficulties, and what you feel your lover can do about them.

Your partner will get the message.

● This method of working is very simple, but you do have to trust that you yourself are an able transmitter. Often we do not realize how difficult communication can be, and here you are trying to make your partner understand how you feel, not to change them.

Confidence in
social situations

Charm bags are a very efficient way of carrying reminders that can add extra zest to life. This one is used to help you overcome shyness, perhaps when you are meeting new people or doing something you have never done before. The spell is best done during the Waxing Moon.

YOU WILL NEED
- ✦ SMALL DRAWSTRING BAG, ABOUT 1–2 IN (2.5–5 CM) DEEP (YOU COULD USE A COLOUR SUCH AS YELLOW TO ENHANCE COMMUNICATION)
- ☽ GROUND NUTMEG
- ● PINE NEEDLES
- ◗ DRIED LAVENDER
- ⚡ PIECE OF MANDRAKE ROOT

METHOD

Put a pinch or two of the nutmeg, pine needles, dried lavender and mandrake root in the bag and tie it closed.

Consecrate and charge the bag during the waxing phase of the Moon so that you can use positive energy.

Wear the bag around your neck or keep it in your pocket.

You should feel a surge of energy whenever you are in a social situation that you find difficult to handle.

When you feel you no longer have need of the support your bag gives you, you can scatter the herbs to the four winds or burn them.

● It is the consecrating of the bag that turns it into a tool for use in everyday situations, so choose your words carefully to express your particular need. Try to approach one new person every day or go into one new situation until you lose your fear.

To create
 opportunities for love

**This is not a spell to draw a person to you, but more to
'open the way' – to alert another person to the possibility
of a relationship with you. The spell should be performed
on a Friday. The use of your mother's ring is symbolic
of continuity.**

 YOU WILL NEED
- ✦ WINE GLASS
- ☽ RING (TRADITIONALLY YOUR MOTHER'S WEDDING RING
  WOULD BE USED)
- ● RED SILK RIBBON, ABOUT 30 IN (80 CM) LONG

METHOD

Put the wine glass the right way up on a table.

Make a pendulum by suspending the ring from the red
silk ribbon.

Hold the pendulum steady by resting your elbow on the
table, with the ribbon between your thumb and forefinger.

Let the ring hang in the mouth of the wine glass.

Clearly say your name, followed by that of the
other person.

Repeat their name twice, i.e. three times in all.

Then, thinking of them, spell their name out loud.

Allow the ring to swing and tap against the wine glass once
for each letter of their name.

Tie the ribbon around your neck, allowing the ring to hang
down over your head.

Wear it for three weeks, and repeat the spell every Friday
for three weeks.

By the end of the third week, the person you have in your sights will show an interest, unless it is not meant to be.

● Let's assume there is someone in whom you are interested, but the interest does not seem to be reciprocated. This spell ensures there are no hindrances, but there has to be at least some feeling for it to stand a chance of working.

 *Friendship*

This spell calls on several disciplines: candle, representational and incantation. You can work it at the time of the New Moon, since you are attempting to bring about new ways of relating to people and also hoping to meet new friends.

 YOU WILL NEED
- ★ SEVERAL SHEETS OF PAPER
- ☽ PEN
- ● JASMINE, LAVENDER OR PATCHOULI ESSENTIAL OIL IN A CARRIER OIL SUCH AS ALMOND
- ◐ WHITE CANDLE

 METHOD

Anoint the candle with a few drops of the oil.

Inscribe it with the Ogham Stave for friendship, Ur:

Light the candle, then take a ritual cleansing bath.

Anoint yourself with more of the oil, paying particular attention to the pulse spots.

Take a sheet of paper and draw a figure to represent yourself – it does not have to be good art.

Make sure your gender is recognizable.

Write underneath the figure all those attributes that make you a good companion, e.g. funny, bubbly, curious etc.

On the other pieces of paper, draw representations of both men and women and the interests you would like them to have which are similar to yours.

Briefly hold between your hands the paper that represents you together with each of the other papers, making sure that the drawings face one another.

Say each time:

 Let us meet each other

Let us greet each other

Let us become friends

Let us become companions

And if we grow to love one another

Then so be it.

Put a drop of oil on one corner of each of the papers.

Now spread the papers out in front of you and visualize a link from you to each of the others, almost like a spider's web.

Say:

 Spider Woman, Spider Woman, weave me a charm

Make me good enough, clever enough them all to disarm.

Let the candle burn out.

You should find that new friends appear before the next New Moon.

● All life can be seen as a network, and each individual is a strand within that network. Spider Woman is a North American goddess who weaves charms and reveals the power and the purpose of each strand. She keeps you aware of the importance of these connections in your life.

To beckon a person

This is a very simple method of putting out a vibration which, if a relationship has a chance of succeeding, will make the other person aware of you. It does not force the other person to do anything, but simply paves the way.

METHOD
Say the following:

 Know I move to you
As you move to me.

As I think of you,
Think also of me.

As I call your name,
Call me to you.
Come to me in love.

Say the person's name three times (if known).

• You may need to recite the whole spell several times in order to feel the proper effect. You might also need to remember that a loving friend is just as important as a friendly lover.

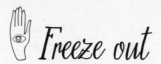# Freeze out

There are many ways of 'freezing people out', and this one which uses ice is good since it will only last as long as the ice remains frozen. The spell should only be used to prevent harm to yourself and others, not to bring harm to anyone else. It is only used if you know the name of the person involved. A good time to do this spell would be with the Waning Moon.

 YOU WILL NEED
- MAGICALLY CHARGED PAPER AND PEN
- WATER IN A BOWL

 METHOD

Write the name of the person concerned in the middle of the paper.

Fold the paper away from you at least four times, all the while sensing the person's influence waning.

Dunk the paper in the water until it is well soaked.

Leave it overnight if necessary.

Put the wet paper into your freezer or ice-making compartment.

Leave it there until you feel the danger is over.

Then release the spell by taking the paper out of the freezer and using words such as:

 All danger passed

   I set you free.

Dispose of the paper in any way you wish.

• You must never forget to set the other person free, lest you find yourself bound to them for longer than is healthy for either of you. By the laws of cause and effect, you must ensure that your actions do not rebound on you.

For a lover to come to you

This spell is reputed to work very quickly, so don't be too impetuous. It is of course a candle spell. Red candles represent passion, so you must take responsibility for whatever happens when you call your lover to you.

YOU WILL NEED
✶ 2 SILVER PINS
☽ RED CANDLE

METHOD

Stick two silver pins through the middle of a red candle at midnight.

Concentrate on your lover.

Repeat their name several times.

After the candle burns down to the pins, your lover will arrive.

It is also said that if you give your lover one of the pins, they will remain bound to you.

If you wish companionship rather than passion, use a candle of a colour that is appropriate to the other person's astrological sign.

● This spell is designed to influence someone else, so be very careful how you use it. Pins were often used in magical work in times gone by because they were readily available. One old custom was to ask a bride for the pins from her wedding dress, for which you were supposed to give her a penny.

In a true you-and-I relationship, we are present mindfully, non-intrusively, the way we are present with things in nature. We do not tell a birch tree it should be more like an elm. We face it with no agenda, only an appreciation that becomes participation: 'I love looking at this birch' becomes 'I am this birch' and then 'I and this birch are opening to a mystery that transcends and holds us both.'

David Richo

To achieve your heart's desire

**This is quite an effective spell and also gives you
something to do while you are waiting for true love.
It makes use of plant magic and candles. Timing is
important because the spell uses the rising of the sun,
as is colour (red to represent passion).**

 YOU WILL NEED

✦ FRESH ROSE (PREFERABLY RED AND PERFUMED)
🕯 2 RED CANDLES

METHOD

Find out the time of the next sunrise.

Just before going to sleep, place a red candle on either side
of the rose.

The next morning at sunrise, take the rose outside.

Hold the rose in front of you and say:

 This red rose is for true love.

True love come to me.

Now go back inside and put the rose between the candles
again.

Light the candles and visualize love burning in the heart of
the one you want.

Keep the candles burning day and night, until the rose
fades.

When the rose is dead, pinch out the candles and then
bury the rose.

• There are many spells for love, and this one is extremely
simple, except that it requires some effort to get up early in
the morning. The concentration that you put into it as you
burn the candles focuses your mind on the matter in hand.

To forget about an ex-lover

This spell is best done at the time of the Waning Moon or New Moon. It is not used to get rid of an old partner, but to exorcize your bad feelings about them. For this reason, it is sensible to finish the spell by sending loving thoughts to your former partner. Woody nightshade is poisonous and you may not care to use it, in which case you can use a bulb of garlic instead.

 YOU WILL NEED
- ✦ PHOTOGRAPH OF YOUR EX-PARTNER
- ☽ SUITABLE CONTAINER FOR BURNING THE PHOTOGRAPH (ONE IN WHICH THE ASHES CAN BE SAVED)
- ● ROOT OF BITTERSWEET (WOODY NIGHTSHADE, WHICH IS POISONOUS)
- ◖ RED CLOTH OR BAG

 METHOD

Place the picture of your ex-partner in the container.

Set it alight.

Gather up all your hurt and pain as the picture burns down.

Feel them flowing away from you as you say these words or similar:

Leave my heart and leave me free,

Leave my life, no pain for me.

As this picture burns to dust,

Help me now, move on I must.

Repeat the words until the picture is burnt out.

Take the herb root and hold it to your solar plexus.

Allow the bad feelings to flow into the root.

Touch the root to your forehead, indicating that you have converted the bad feelings to good.

Wrap everything, including the container of ashes, in your red bag or cloth.

As soon as convenient, bury it as far away from your home as possible.

• If you have had a relationship that is argumentative and turned nasty, it is often better to end it and move on. This is of course your choice, but if you wish to try again, you may like to try the spell 'To stop an argument' (pages 110–11).

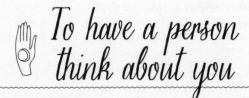

To have a person think about you

This spell is designed to take effect over time. Generally, a relationship that grows slowly has more chance of success than a whirlwind romance, and the former is what is represented here. Small seeds represent the many facets of a relationship, and this spell is best done as the Moon is growing in power.

 YOU WILL NEED
- ✦ PACKET OF SEEDS OF YOUR CHOICE
- ☽ POT OF SOIL (TO GROW THE SEEDS)
- • SMALL COPPER OBJECT SUCH AS A PENNY (COPPER IS SACRED TO VENUS, THE GODDESS OF LOVE)

 METHOD

On a night when the Moon is waxing, go outside and hold the penny in the moonlight.

Bury the penny in the soil in the pot.

Sprinkle the seeds on top, forming the initial of the other person's name.

As the seeds germinate, love should also grow.

Remember that just as plants need nurturing, so too does love, so you will need to look after your growing seeds.

• It is said that the plants will grow and flourish if the love is meant to be, but will wither and die if there is no real energy in the relationship. For those who are not very good at plant care, you might choose to put a reminder to nurture your plants somewhere prominent.

To have your love returned

This spell uses candle magic and is also representational. It is a little more complicated than most other spells because it requires an understanding of symbolism. The objects need not be the real things, but they can be miniaturizations such as cake decorations. The spell is best done on a Friday.

YOU WILL NEED
- ✦ PINK CANDLE
- ☽ BLUE CANDLE
- • GOLD CANDLE (TO REPRESENT THE RELATIONSHIP)
- ◖ HORSESHOE (TO REPRESENT LUCK IN LOVE)
- ⚡ KEY (TO REPRESENT THE KEY TO YOUR HEART)
- ◗ 2 ROSES
- ◖ ARTICLE OF YOUR LOVE INTEREST'S CLOTHING (FAILING THAT, YOU CAN USE SOMETHING OF YOUR OWN)

METHOD

Light the pink and blue candles (pink first if you are female; blue if male), followed by the gold.

Place the horseshoe and key on either side of the candles, with the roses between them.

When the candles have burnt down, wrap the flowers, key and horseshoe in the clothing.

Place the items in a bedroom drawer and leave them alone for 14 days.

If the flowers are still fresh after 14 days, this is a good sign.

You should then bury them or put them (along with the horseshoe and key) in a pot-pourri.

• You might use this spell when you think a relationship with someone would be worthwhile. If you cannot find an article of the other person's clothing, a handkerchief or some other small article will do just as well. If that is not possible, then use a square of pink material.

To heal a rift

This Romany spell works on the principle of making two things (or halves) one. The apple has always been a symbol for love, and pins are a symbol of industriousness, denoting the effort that must be put into a marriage or relationship.

YOU WILL NEED
- ✴ FRESH APPLE
- ☽ CLEAN SHEET OF WHITE PAPER
- ● PEN
- ◗ KNIFE
- ⚡ 2 PINS, COCKTAIL STICKS OR TWIGS

 METHOD

Cut the apple in half.

Tradition says it is helpful, but not vital, if the seeds remain whole. If they don't, reconciliation may simply be a little bit more difficult to bring about.

Write one person's name on the paper. Next to it, write the other person's name. Ensure that the space taken up by the names does not exceed the width of the halved apple.

Cut out the names.

Place the paper with the names between the two halves of the apple.

Visualize the marriage or relationship being healed.

Skewer the apple halves together, inserting the pins or twigs diagonally from right to left, and then vice versa.

If you are healing your own relationship, send your love to the person concerned and ask to receive their love in return.

If the spell is for someone else, visualize the couple surrounded by a pink cloud or aura in a loving embrace.

• Divorce is disliked among the Romanies even today. When action is required to heal a seemingly irreparable rift, this spell can begin a process of reconciliation. To finish off the spell, Romanies use their campfire to bake the apple until it appears whole.

To strengthen attraction

If you love someone but feel they are not reciprocating, try this spell. Be aware, though, that by using it you are trying to have a direct effect upon the other person. This is an example of representational magic because the hair stands for the person you are hoping to influence.

 YOU WILL NEED
+ A FEW STRANDS OF THE PERSON'S HAIR
⟩ ROSE-SCENTED INCENSE STICK

 METHOD
Light the incense.

Repeat the name of the one you long for, saying each time:

[Name], love me now.

Hold the hair on the burning incense until it frizzles away.

As the hair burns, think of the person's indifference dissipating and being replaced by passion.

Leave the incense to burn out.

• Before you perform this spell, you should have tried to work out why the other person feels indifferent and consider whether what you are proposing is appropriate. For instance, if the person you want to attract has not learnt how to commit to a relationship, it would be unfair to try to influence them.

 # *To stop an argument*

This is a spell to stop an argument between you and another person, or to change their feelings of aggravation. You are using colour and representational magic here. So that you do not let your own feelings intrude, you might take a ritual bath first.

 YOU WILL NEED
- ✦ GLASS PLATE (DEEP PURPLE IF POSSIBLE, BUT IF NOT, CLEAR WILL WORK TOO)
- ◗ PHOTOGRAPH OF THE PERSON WITH WHOM YOU HAVE ARGUED

METHOD

The plate is used for two reasons. Firstly, being glass, it reflects back to the person; and secondly, through its colour, it raises the whole question to its highest vibration.

Place the photograph face down on the plate for no more than 15 minutes.

You do not want to over-influence the recipient, so spend a few moments remembering the good times you have had.

For this reason, if using an old-fashioned film print, you should also be aware of where the negative is, so that you are only using positive energy.

The person will either call or drop in in no more than 24 hours later, so you can resolve your difficulties.

If they do not, repeat the procedure for no more than 15 minutes.

If you still haven't heard from them after a third time, give them a phone call or visit them, because their feelings will have changed.

You will then know that you have done all you can to be on good terms with them.

• It is often difficult to get back onto a normal footing with a person after an argument, so be prepared to apologize for any part that you have had in the difficulty. Remember that you are only dealing with that particular argument, not deeper issues within the friendship.

Nether garment spell for fidelity

This spell uses a combination of nutmeg and intimate garments in a form of sympathetic magic together with herbal magic. It is said to keep a partner faithful. It can be done at any time, particularly when you suspect that your partner may be open to temptation.

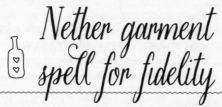

YOU WILL NEED
- ✶ 2 WHOLE NUTMEGS
- ☽ A PAIR OF YOUR CLEAN UNDERWEAR, AND A PAIR OF YOUR PARTNER'S
- ● WIDE RED RIBBON
- ◖ LARGE WHITE ENVELOPE
- ⚡ PIN OR YOUR BURIN

METHOD

Using the pin or your burin, carefully scratch your partner's initial on one nutmeg and your own on the other.

Tie them together with the ribbon.

Wrap them in the underwear and then place in the envelope.

Sleep with the envelope under your pillow if your partner is away or you are separated from them.

● At one time, nutmeg was the most expensive spice available, so one would have to be fairly serious about a relationship to be willing to lock away such a valuable commodity. This spell is not to be entered into lightly, nor designed to keep someone with you against their will.

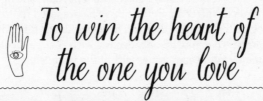

To win the heart of the one you love

This is an old folklore spell. The bulb is a symbol of love growing unseen and unrecognized for a time, finally flowering at the right time. You cannot simply leave it alone, but must tend to it if it is to grow successfully.

YOU WILL NEED
- ✦ ONION BULB
- ☽ NEW FLOWER POT
- ● EARTH OR COMPOST
- ◗ YOUR BURIN

METHOD
Scratch the name of the one you love on the base of the bulb with your burin.

Plant it in earth or compost in the pot.

Place the pot on a windowsill, if possible facing the direction in which your sweetheart lives.

Over the bulb, repeat the name of the one you desire morning and night until the bulb takes root, begins to shoot and finally blooms.

Say the following incantation whenever you think of the other person:

 May its roots grow,

May its leaves grow,

May its flowers grow,

And as it does so,

[Name of person]'s love grow.

• You need patience for this spell, and you may well find that you lose the impetus for the relationship before the spell is complete. If so, this would suggest the relationship may not be right for you.

To rid yourself of an unwanted admirer

Occasionally people get into a situation where they are being pursued by someone whose attention is a nuisance. Rather than reacting in anger, it is often easier to open the way for the unwanted suitor to leave. This spell, done on a Waning Moon – that is, after the Full Moon and before the next New Moon – often does the trick.

 YOU WILL NEED
- ✦ VERVAIN LEAVES
- ☽ FIERCE FIRE

METHOD

Light a fire.

Pick up the vervain and as you do so, call out the name of the offending person.

Fling the leaves on the fire and say:

 Withdraw from me now I need you not.

(There is a requirement to declaim passionately and to use some force in any spell that is designed to drive someone away from you. Therefore, be very sure that you do not wish this person to be in your life in any way.)

Repeat the action three nights in a row.

● Preferably this spell should be done outside, but it can be also be performed indoors if you have a suitable fireplace and provided that you are careful. Strictly, one is supposed to gather the vervain leaves, although with urban living this is a bit of a tall order. Make sure you have at least a couple of handfuls of the dried herb.

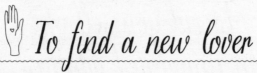

To find a new lover

This spell works best if it is done at the time of the New Moon. Everything you use should be brand new so that you can change the vibration and look forward to the future with hope. The spell is representational and best done at the time of the New Moon.

 YOU WILL NEED
- ✦ HEART-SHAPED ROSE PETAL, OR A RED HEART CUT OUT OF PAPER OR CARD
- ☽ CLEAN SHEET OF WHITE PAPER
- ● NEW PEN
- ◗ NEW CANDLE (PREFERABLY PINK)
- ⚡ NEW ENVELOPE

 METHOD
On the day of a New Moon, take a heart-shaped rose petal or cut a red heart out of paper or card.

Take a clean sheet of white paper and, with the new pen, write on it:

 As this heart shines in candlelight,

I draw you to me tonight.

Bathe and change into nightclothes.

When ready, light the candle and read the invocation out loud.

Hold the heart in front of the flame and let the candlelight shine onto it.

Place the heart and spell in a new envelope.

Seal it with wax from the candle.

Conceal the envelope and leave it untouched for one cycle of the Moon (28 days).

By the time the Moon is new again, there should be new love in your life.

• So many people need companionships and partnership in order to boost their feelings of self-worth. But to do a spell like this means, as always, that one must be willing to take on everything that a partnership brings.

A lover's token

This bottle is good to give to your lover as a token of your love and to intensify the link between you. The herbs are all well known for their association with love, and the link between the bottles should help you to communicate.

YOU WILL NEED

FOR EACH TOKEN:
- ✦ GLASS BOTTLE WITH CORK (ANY SIZE WILL DO)
- ◗ HANDFUL OF CRUSHED, DRIED ROSE PETALS (PREFERABLY FROM FLOWERS GIVEN BY YOUR LOVER)
- ● DRIED/FRESH ROSEMARY (FOR LOVE AND STRENGTH)
- ◖ DRIED/FRESH LAVENDER
- ⚡ ROSE OIL OR WATER
- ◗ WAX (PINK OR RED IS GOOD FOR LOVE)
- ◖ PINK RIBBON

METHOD

Crush the rose petals and place in the bottles. Put in the rosemary and/or lavender, then add the oil or rose water almost to the top, leaving some room for air to circulate. Cork the bottle and drip wax over the cork to seal the bottle.

Lay the ribbon on a flat surface. Place one bottle at either end of the ribbon. Gradually move them towards one another along the ribbon, to signify you coming together with your lover.

When they meet, tie the ribbon around your partner's bottle and give it to them.

Place your bottle on a shelf, dresser or anywhere where it will not be disturbed.

● These bottles are tangible evidence of the link between you and your lover. You may use them to remind you of the good times or soothe you in the bad. The ribbon signifies the link between you, so whenever you think of it, you have immediately connected.

Respond; don't react.
Listen; don't talk.
Think; don't assume.

Raji Lukkoor

Herbal charm to attract love

This is a charm that uses a combination of colour, herbs and knots in its fashioning. Love is always of interest, but do remember that you need to be clear in your aspirations. Numbers are also used, seven being a particularly potent one.

YOU WILL NEED
* ✦ ACACIA, ROSE, MYRTLE, JASMINE OR LAVENDER PETALS (IN ANY COMBINATION OR SINGLY)
* ❥ RED HEART CUT OUT FROM PAPER OR FELT
* ● COPPER COIN OR RING
* ◗ CIRCLE OF ROSE- OR RED-COLOURED CLOTH
* ⚡ BLUE THREAD OR RIBBON

METHOD
Place the petals, heart and coin or ring on the cloth and visualize the type of lover you are looking for.

Tie the cloth into a pouch with the blue thread or ribbon, using seven knots.

As you tie the knots, you may chant an incantation such as:

Seven knots I tie above,

Seven knots for me and love.

Hang the pouch close to your pillow and await the results.

● This charm is designed to draw someone towards you, but it does not guarantee that you will necessarily fall madly in love with the person who comes along – you have simply made yourself attractive to them. If the person isn't right for you, be prepared to let them down gently.

Love charm

This spell uses herbal magic together with the elements. It comes from an age when every spell maker would use what was easily available to them. The best time for performing it is around the time of the New Moon.

 YOU WILL NEED
- ✦ LARGE STRIP OF BIRCH BARK (GATHERED AT THE TIME OF THE NEW MOON)
- ☽ RED INK
- ● PEN WITH A NIB
- ◖ GRANULAR ROSE OR JASMINE LOVE INCENSE
- ⚡ CONTAINER SUITABLE FOR BURNING GRANULAR INCENSE

METHOD

Write on the birch strip:

 Bring me true love.

Burn the birch bark along with the incense in the container, and say:

 Goddess of Love, God of Desire,

Bring to me sweet passion's fire.

The above uses the element of fire.

To use water, cast the bark into a stream or other flowing water, and say:

 Message of love, I set you free

To capture a love and return to me.

● Birch highlights the recognition of the change in mindset from maiden to mother, and indicates to the universe that you are ready to take on the responsibility of partnership. You should not use this charm unless you are prepared to take on that responsibility.

To obtain love
 from a specific person

This spell uses fire as its vehicle – not as candle magic, but in your cauldron. It involves an incantation and you can also use magical ink and parchment if you wish. The spell is best done at night-time, and the power of the number three is not just for lust, but also for love.

 YOU WILL NEED
- ✦ YOUR CAULDRON OR A FIREPROOF CONTAINER
- ☾ PIECE OF PAPER
- ● PEN AND RED INK
- ♦ FRAGRANT WOOD OR HERBS TO BURN (YOU COULD USE APPLE, BIRCH AND CEDAR)

METHOD

Light a small fire in your cauldron or container.

Cut out a piece of paper that is 3 x 3 in (7.5 x 7.5 cm).

With the pen and red ink, draw a heart on the paper and colour it in.

Write the name of the person that you desire on the heart three times. If you wish, do this from the edge to the middle in a spiral, to signify how deep your love goes.

While writing, think of the person's heart burning with desire for you, just like the flames of the fire.

Kiss the names on the heart three times.

Place the paper in the fire while saying the following words three times:

 Soon my love will come to me
This I know that it must be
Fire comes from this wood

Bring love and caring that it would

Make our hearts glow and shine,

Bringing love that shall be mine.

Sit quietly as the paper burns, visualizing your lover coming towards you.

After you are finished, concentrate for a few minutes, then extinguish the fire.

Say quietly three times:

 So, let it be.

• Do not get impatient if nothing happens for a while. Simply have confidence that you will be given an opportunity to have a relationship with this particular person. How you handle the relationship thereafter is entirely up to you.

To bring someone into your life

This spell can be used to attract love or to draw a companion closer. It should be started on the night of a New Moon. It is representational in that the cruet set suggests a pairing, and it also uses colour.

 YOU WILL NEED
- SALT AND PEPPER SHAKERS (OR ANY TWO OBJECTS THAT OBVIOUSLY MAKE A PAIR)
- LENGTH OF PINK RIBBON, ABOUT 3 FT (1 M) LONG

 METHOD
Assign the salt shaker (or other article) as one person and the pepper shaker (or other article) as the other.

Take the piece of pink ribbon, and tie one object to one end and the other object to the other end, leaving a good length of ribbon between them.

Every morning, untie the ribbon, move the objects a little closer together, and retie the knots.

Eventually the objects will touch.

Leave them bound together for seven days before untying them.

By this time, love should have entered your life.

● There are several spells that make use of the idea that two people must travel along a set path. This one signifies the path of love. In the tying and untying of the ribbon, it also suggests the freedoms that exist in the relationship.

To rekindle your lover's interest

This technique is worth trying when your lover is not paying you enough attention. The laurel leaves are used to back up the energy that you are putting into making the relationship work. This spell uses herbal and elemental magic.

 YOU WILL NEED
✴ LARGE QUANTITY OF LAUREL LEAVES
☾ A FIRE

 METHOD
Sit in front of the embers of a fire and gaze into them, concentrating on your lover.

Keep your gaze fixed into the fire.

With your left hand, throw some laurel leaves onto the embers.

As they burn, say:

 Laurel leaves burn into the fire,

Bring to me my heart's desire.

Wait until the flames die down, then do the same again.

Repeat the actions once more.

It is said that within 24 hours your lover will come back to you.

• This spell must allow the person who you are targeting to have choices. To keep your partner by your side if they are unhappy would not be right. The method allows you to give careful consideration as to the amount of fidelity and security you require within a relationship. This spell is similar to 'To rid yourself of an unwanted admirer' (pages 113–14), and demonstrates how different herbs used in similar ways can bring about different results.

Resolving a love triangle

Sometimes it is possible to get caught up in a situation in which three people are in a love triangle. It would be wrong to influence anyone one way or another, so here is a way of resolving the situation that should not harm anyone. It is best done at the time of the Full Moon.

YOU WILL NEED
✦ 3 LENGTHS OF STRING, EACH ABOUT 3 FT (1 M) LONG
☽ AN OPEN SPACE WHERE YOU WILL NOT BE DISTURBED

METHOD
Form a triangle on the ground with the three pieces of string, so that the ends are just touching.

Step into the middle of the triangle.

Appeal to the Triple Goddess in her guise of Maid, Mother and Crone.

Use words such as:

 Triple Goddess hear my plea,

I ask you now to set us free,

It's not a problem I can alter,

So help me now lest I falter.

These words put you in touch with your own inner self, which means that you make whatever decision is right for you.

Wait for a few moments to allow the energy to build up, then raise your arms in a 'V' shape (the Goddess position) and say:

 So let it be.

Allow yourself time to consider the problem from all perspectives before making a decision as to how you should act.

Each time you consider the position, remember to repeat the first two lines of the verse above.

• It usually takes a little time for a situation like this to reach some kind of resolution, but this spell allows you to feel supported and cared for. Gradually it will become apparent as to the action you must take, and you can accept that it is the ultimately the best outcome for everyone concerned.

To ease a broken heart

This spell contains many of the types of magic normally used in spells: it features candle, herbal and plant magic, as well as representational magic. The technique is designed to make you feel better rather than have an effect on anyone else.

 YOU WILL NEED

- ✦ STRAWBERRY TEABAG
- ☽ SMALL WAND, OR A STICK FROM A WILLOW TREE
- ● SEA SALT
- ◖ 2 PINK CANDLES
- ⚡ MIRROR
- ◗ PINK DRAWSTRING BAG
- ◖ QUARTZ CRYSTAL
- ♥ COPPER PENNY
- ✦ BOWL MADE OF CHINA OR CRYSTAL THAT IS SPECIAL TO YOU
- ◗ 1 TEASPOON DRIED JASMINE
- ℮ 1 TEASPOON ORRIS-ROOT POWDER
- ▼ 1 TEASPOON STRAWBERRY LEAVES
- ✱ 1 TEASPOON YARROW
- ○ 10 DROPS (AT LEAST) APPLE-BLOSSOM OIL OR PEACH OIL
- ◆ 10 DROPS (AT LEAST) STRAWBERRY OIL

 METHOD

Charge all the ingredients before you begin.

On a Friday morning or evening (the day sacred to the Goddess Venus), take a bath in sea salt in the light of a pink candle.

As you dry off and dress, sip the strawberry tea.

Use a dab of strawberry oil as perfume or cologne.

Apply makeup or groom yourself to look your best.

Cast a circle with the willow wand around a table on which the other ingredients have been placed.

Light the second pink candle.

Mix all the oils and herbs in the bowl.

While you stir, look at yourself in the mirror and say:

 Oh, Great Mother Earth,

 Nurture and protect me now,

 Let me use the strengths I know I have.

Look into the mirror after you have finished mixing the ingredients and say:

 Mother of all things,

 All that is great is mine,

 Help me now to be the person I can be

 And let me overcome my difficulty.

Put half the mixture in the pink bag and add the penny and crystal.

Carry the bag with you until you feel you no longer need it.

Leave the other half of the potion in the bowl in a room where you will smell the fragrance. Repeat this ritual every Friday, if you wish.

• Unfortunately, the breakup of a relationship can truly knock our confidence. This spell is designed to restore yours as quickly as possible. It does not matter who is right or wrong; what is important is simply that you are able to go forward with dignity.

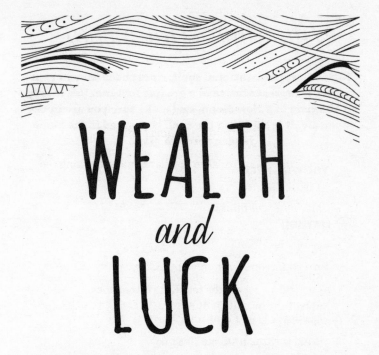

WEALTH

and

LUCK

It may seem like mindfulness and money have nothing to do with each other, but in fact our state of mind does affect our bank balance, as well as the tendency to attract luck into our lives. This chapter shows how to cast spells that will change your financial thinking and shift your consciousness towards prosperity instead of mere survival. From banishing your debts to drawing money towards you, there are many mindful spells that will reward you in all sorts of ways.

Attracting extra money

This is a representational spell, since the money in your pocket is representative of a greater fortune. Use it only at the time of a New Moon, and make sure you are in the open air. It is said that the spell is negated if the Moon is seen through glass.

 YOU WILL NEED
+ LOOSE CHANGE

METHOD

Gaze at the Moon.

Turn your money over in your pocket.

As you do so, repeat the following three times:

Goddess of Light and Love, I pray

Bring fortune unto me this day.

You will know that the spell has worked when you find extra money in your pocket or purse, or if you come across money unexpectedly.

• In previous times, the Moon was recognized as much as the Sun as being the bringer of good luck. This spell acknowledges that and allows you to make use of her power. It is said to ensure that you have at least enough money for bed and board until the next New Moon.

Your vision will become clear only when you look into your heart. Who looks outside, dreams. Who looks inside, awakens.

Carl Jung

Fast luck oil

The oil used here contains herbal essences, all of which have the effect of quickening up a spell. However, there is need for a word of warning, as many people nowadays have sensitivities to so many substances. If ingested internally, wintergreen is highly toxic, so you should be careful when dealing with it; and cinnamon oil can irritate the skin. When used to dress a candle, however, the combined oils are a speedy way of making things happen.

 YOU WILL NEED
- ✦ SMALL BOTTLE
- ◗ 10 DROPS WINTERGREEN OIL
- ● 10 DROPS VANILLA OIL
- ◗ 10 DROPS CINNAMON OIL
- ⚡ CARRIER SUCH AS ALMOND OIL
- ◗ IF YOU WISH, YOU CAN SUSPEND A SMALL PIECE OF ALKANET ROOT (BLOODROOT) IN THE BOTTLE FOR A DEEP RED COLOUR AND EXTRA POWER
- ◖ FOR MONEY SPELLS, YOU CAN ALSO ADD GOLD OR SILVER GLITTER

 METHOD

Carefully combine the essential and carrier oils in the bottle.

Shake well, and repeat the following words as you do so at least three times:

Fast Luck, Fast Luck

Bring to me my desire.

Now add the other ingredients, if you are using them, and leave the bottle in a cool, dark place for at least 24 hours for the oils to blend.

After this time, use the oil to dress your candles.

As you are drawing luck towards you, remember that you should dress the candle from the top down.

If you are using this oil for a money spell, concentrate on money coming towards you, use a green candle and repeat the words above.

Use a brown candle if you have a business deal you need to accelerate, but this time it is wise to add a few flakes of silver or gold glitter.

To bring love into your life, use a pink candle, visualize your ideal person coming into your life and repeat the words above, adding at the end:

 If it be right for all concerned.

Let the candles burn out safely.

- You should have some indication that this routine is working within about 36 hours. If there is no effect, then you must consider what obstacles there are to your progress. These may have come to light since you began the spell, and you can attempt to remove them before carrying out the procedure again.

Footwash for money

This is a folklore recipe, and would strictly only become a spell if an incantation or invocation were added. Black Cohosh is probably best known as a herb to be used at the time of the menopause, but here it is used as a footwash that will lead you to money.

YOU WILL NEED
- ✦ BLACK COHOSH ROOT
- ☽ CUP OF BOILING WATER
- ● SMALL BOTTLE

METHOD

Soak the root in the cup of boiling water for 15 minutes.

Strain the water and throw away the root.

Put the liquid in the bottle for seven days and leave it alone.

On the eighth day, rub the liquid all over the bottom of your shoes.

Be alert to your own intuition until money comes your way.

● It is said that you will either find money, win it, or gain it in some legal manner. The spell cannot be used to acquire a specific amount, but you can bear in mind what your needs are.

Money spell

This is a spell to help you come to terms with money and your attitude to it, and should be performed around the time of the Full Moon. There are two versions of the spell: one using play money and another using real money. Choose whichever you are most comfortable with.

YOU WILL NEED

✦ GREEN TAPER CANDLE

☽ MINT OR HONEYSUCKLE OIL

● PLAY MONEY OF VARIOUS DENOMINATIONS, OR A SINGLE NOTE OF THE LARGEST DENOMINATION OF REAL MONEY THAT YOU CAN AFFORD

METHOD

Two days before the Full Moon, take the green candle to your sacred space. Carve several currency symbols on the candle, thinking of a more prosperous life as you do so.

Anoint the candle with the essential oil. Place it in the holder and set it in your sacred space. Light the candle.

IF USING PLAY MONEY:

Spread out your 'money' in front of the burning candle Handle it, sort it and play with it. Spend at least 5–10 minutes thinking about your attitude to money, and how you would use it if it were real.

Then extinguish the candle.

The next night, light the candle again. Play with the money again, thinking about how you might make it grow.

After 10–15 minutes, extinguish the candle.

The third night, the night of the Full Moon, do the same again; think about how you would help others.

Before the candle burns out completely, burn a large denomination note of your play money after you have finished sorting it. This is your offering to the Gods, but it also represents your acknowledgement that money is simply an energy to be used.

IF USING REAL MONEY:

The ritual is the same except that during your meditation on the first day you should think about how you wish to spend the money you are going to accrue.

During the second ritual, visualize your money growing and becoming more. See yourself going to the bank to put it into your account or some such action.

On the third night, you have a choice. You can either burn the money, place it somewhere safe – perhaps on your altar as a reminder of your good fortune – or give it to charity.

It is important that you do not use it for your own purposes.

• This spell does require a certain amount of courage, but having the confidence to take a risk and burn money – play or real – really can open up your mind to the opportunities for prosperity.

Start living right here, in each present moment. When we stop dwelling on the past or worrying about the future, we're open to rich sources of information we've been missing out on – information that can keep us out of the downward spiral and poised for a richer life.

Mark Williams

Eliminating personal poverty

A modern-day adaptation of an ancient formula, this spell ensures that you always have the necessities of life, such as somewhere to stay and enough to eat. Because it becomes part of your everyday environment, you simply need to refresh the ingredients when you feel the time is right.

YOU WILL NEED
* SMALL GLASS CONTAINER CONTAINING EQUAL QUANTITIES OF:
  * SALT
  * SUGAR
  * RICE
* SAFETY PIN

METHOD

Fill the container with a mixture of the salt, sugar and rice.

Place the open safety pin in the centre of the mixture.

Put the container in the open air where you can easily see it.

Occasionally give the container a shake to reinvigorate the energies.

• Although this spell has no particular time frame, the more confident you become in your own abilities, the quicker it will work. Rather than using salt, sugar and rice, you could use a pot-pourri of your choice. Shaking the container also keeps the energies fresh, and you must use your intuition as to when the ingredients need changing.

Silver spell

This spell relies on the use of candles, and takes about a week to perform. Before you begin, believe you have prosperity and that you have no money worries. Consider your attitude to money. You will probably find that the spell is best begun on a Friday.

 YOU WILL NEED
- ✳ SMALL BOWL
- ☽ 7 SILVER COINS
- ● GREEN CANDLE AND HOLDER

METHOD

Place the bowl and the candle and its holder on a flat surface in your home, where it will be passed every day.

For the next seven days, put a coin in the bowl.

After seven days, take the candle in your hands and imagine prosperity coming to you. Sense the opportunities that you will have with money. Be aware of the energy that has been given to money.

Place the candle in the holder.

Pour the seven coins into your left hand. Draw a circle with your hand around the coins.

Put the first coin right in front of the candle. As you place it, say these or similar words:

 Money grow, make it mine
Money flow, money's mine.

Place the other coins around the candle one by one, and repeat the incantation.

Finally, light the candle and allow it to burn out.

Leave the money in position for at least three days. It is better if you do not spend this money, if possible.

• This spell is designed for long-term security. Just as you build the energy very slowly, so the gains will build slowly too. A variation of the spell is to take a scallop shell which represents the Great Mother, and place the coins in that, leaving them as an offering.

Removing misfortune

This spell uses plant magic combined with folk magic and the meaning of numbers. Burying an object binds the energy of what it represents, and reciting prayers raises the vibration to the point where any negativity is nullified. The instruction 'within sight of a church' suggests that the bad luck then is overseen by the angels.

 YOU WILL NEED
- 3 SMALL JARS (HONEY OR BABY FOOD JARS WORK WELL)
- 9 CLOVES OF GARLIC
- 9 THORNS FROM A WHITE ROSE, OR 9 PINS

METHOD
Pierce the cloves with the thorns or pins, saying the following forcefully while doing so:

 Misfortune begone from me.

Put three of the cloves and pins in each jar.

Bury each jar within sight of a church. Say the Lord's prayer each time you do this.

Walk away, and don't look back at what you have done.

• This spell can give impressively fast results. As soon as you become aware of the misfortune you are suffering, look for a common theme – ask yourself whether your problems are financial, love etc – and actually name them in the words you use. Because you have addressed the misfortune three times, it cannot remain.

To banish your debts

This spell uses candle and incense magic and, if you wish, the art of magical writing. You could choose incense or oil for purification or protection – whichever seems right for you. It is suggested that you perform this spell at the time of the Waning Moon, as this can be used to help take away the difficulty.

YOU WILL NEED

- ✦ ROLLED PARCHMENT OR PAPER, 2 IN (5 CM) WIDE AND AS LONG AS YOU LIKE
- ☽ BLACK PEN, OR PEN WITH MAGICAL BLACK INK
- ● PIN OR YOUR BURIN
- ◖ PURPLE CANDLE
- ⚡ UNBREAKABLE CANDLE HOLDER
- ◗ OIL OF YOUR CHOICE
- ◖ INCENSE OF YOUR CHOICE

METHOD

Light the incense and dress the candle with the oil.

List all your debts on the parchment or paper.

Draw a banishing pentagram on the back of the parchment or paper. This is drawn lower left point to top, to lower right, to top left, to top right, and back to lower left:

Carve another banishing pentagram with the pin or burin on the candle.

Place the rolled parchment or paper in the candle holder, then tighten the candle on top.

Do this carefully, as your candle will eventually set the paper alight.

Concentrate on banishing your debts.

Visualize your happiness and relief when the debts are banished.

Light the candle.

Take the candle to the East and ask that the Spirit of Air acknowledges your intention to be debt-free.

Replace the candle in the holder, making sure it is safe to burn out where it stands.

In your own words, ask for your debts to be banished and replaced with prosperity.

Allow the candle to burn out completely, but as it comes to the end, make sure that you are present.

The paper will catch fire and flare up, so it must be properly attended to.

As you do this, be aware of the lifting of the burden of debt.

● You should not expect your debts to simply disappear, but the wherewithal to clear them should come your way quite quickly. This might be, for instance, in the form of an unexpected gift or the opportunity for some extra work. Once your debts are cleared, you are honour-bound not to create the same problems again.

To attract a wealthy male partner

This spell uses symbolism, herbalism, candles and colour to achieve its purpose. The dragon is a symbol of wealth, wisdom, power and nobility, while ginseng is said to enhance virility. The supposition is that by putting all of them together, you create the right vibration for attraction. If performing this the first time, do it at the time of the New Moon.

YOU WILL NEED
- ✦ REPRESENTATION OF A DRAGON (PICTURE, STATUE ETC)
- ☽ PIECE OF GINSENG ROOT OR POWDERED GINSENG
- ● RED CANDLE

METHOD

Light your candle.

Pick up the ginseng root and say:

 By the power of this Man root
I pray for one to come to me
Strong and brave, wise and astute
Funny and loving to look after me.

Then pick up the dragon symbol and say:

Power of the dragon, strong and true
Hear me now as I call to you
Bring me a man that I can love
And one that I can be proud of.

Place the two objects in front of the candle and allow the flame to burn out.

When this is done, place the representation of the dragon on a high shelf to represent status.

Either keep the ginseng root beside your bed, or use the powder as an incense additive until it is used up.

By that time, your new man should have arrived.

• You can use your own form of words to bring the kind of man you want. Be careful, though, as you may get more than you bargained for. To attract a woman would require more feminine symbols such as a fish or a ladybird, and angelica root instead of ginseng.

Winning brass

If you are a gambler and use dice, you may like to try this spell. It uses planetary correspondences and number symbolism. Properly charged, your dice should create the ability to have Lady Luck – one of the manifestations of the Goddess – on your side.

 YOU WILL NEED
- ✴ BRASS DIE (BRASS IS SACRED TO VENUS)
- ☽ WOOD DIE (PERHAPS SYCAMORE, WHICH IS ALSO SACRED TO VENUS, OR ANY OTHER SACRED WOOD), OR IF YOU CANNOT FIND A WOOD DIE, AN ACRYLIC ONE WILL SUFFICE
- ● MONEY INCENSE
- ◗ GREEN CANDLE

 METHOD
You will need to make a dedication of your die before you start.

Use fairly flowery language in order to get the energy flowing.

Say something like:

🪶 🪶 *Oh Lady of the Morning Star*

Come to me here from afar

This cube of chance

Its powers enhance

That it becomes my lodestar.

Now it will depend on its material as to how you wish the spell to work for you.

Brass is a material that traditionally heightens the intuitive powers, so you could use words such as:

🪶 🪶 *So show me now your bounty.*

Sycamore, which signifies love, receptivity and the ability to communicate, or one of the sacred trees such as holly, a symbol of luck, could be dedicated with the words:

🪶 🪶 *Bring your knowledge to me.*

Your acrylic die, far from being inert, can be made magically powerful by intent. Use words such as:

🪶 🪶 *Awaken to the power of gain.*

Light the incense and candle.

Pass each die through the incense smoke and through the candle flame, visualizing yourself winning with your lucky dice.

When you win, always put by a tenth of your winnings for good causes.

• When playing games of chance, it is thought that fingering the brass die will give the information needed to win. Using the other die as your playing piece should ensure some good winnings. If you do not share your good fortune, however, it will not continue.

This isn't just 'another day, another dollar'. It's more like 'another day, another miracle'.

Victoria Moran

Want spell

Since Mother Nature supplies our most basic needs, this spell uses the cycle of her existence to help fulfil your wants. The leaf is representative of her power, and you use natural objects to signify that all things must come to pass.

 YOU WILL NEED
- ✦ MARKER PEN
- ☽ FULLY GROWN LEAF

METHOD

Write or draw on the leaf a word, picture or letter that represents the thing that you want.

Lay the leaf on the ground.

As the leaf withers, it takes your desire to the Earth.

In thanks, Mother Nature will grant your wish.

You may also throw the leaf into running water or place it under a stone, if you wish.

● This method owes a great deal to folk magic and an appreciation of the cycle of growth and decay. In such spells, it is customary to use a leaf that has fallen rather than picking one from a tree. If you do the latter, you should thank the tree for its bounty.

 *String spell*

This representational spell is very simple. It pays homage to the art of knotting, and makes use of your sacred space if you are able to leave your altar in place. Otherwise, simply use a windowsill in sunlight or moonlight.

 YOU WILL NEED
★ LENGTH OF STRING LONG ENOUGH TO OUTLINE YOUR MATERIAL DESIRE

 METHOD

Sit quietly with the piece of string and mentally pour your wish into it.

Try to have a clear picture in your mind of what you want.

Tie a knot in one end of the string, and say:

 With this knot the gods I implore
Bring this [your desire] my way, for sure.

Tie a knot in the other end of the string, and say:

 With this knot I lock it in
With thanks for the gift that it will bring.

Lay the string on a flat surface and fashion it into as close a picture of your material desire as you can.

Leave it in place for at least three days.

When your wish has manifested, don't forget to thank the gods either by giving something to charity or offering your skills to the community in which you live.

● This spell seems to work best if you actually need the object you are representing. The gods do not grant their favours without some effort on your part, so use your gift well. Your relationship with the gods is a two-way street.

Candles and pennies

Fire and finance have a natural affinity, so a candle spell using pennies is a good way of drawing money towards you. Colour is important, and green is traditionally used in money spells. Try this spell on a Friday.

 YOU WILL NEED
- ✦ GREEN CANDLE
- ☽ GLASS TUMBLER
- ● ENOUGH SMALL COINS TO HALF-FILL THE GLASS
- ◖ YOUR BURIN

METHOD

Half-fill the glass with the coins.

Inscribe the candle with the good fortune and completion rune Fehu:

Put the candle in the glass.

Light the candle and let it burn down so that the wax is intermingled with the pennies. As you light the candle, state that you only want what is needed, nothing more.

Place the glass in a safe space to burn out. There is a slight risk that as the glass gets hot it may shatter, but the pennies should absorb most of the heat.

● This method is based on the idea that money will 'stick' to you. Hopefully, having done the spell once, you will not need to do it again. A variation on this spell is to manifest objects that you need by inscribing the candle with a picture of what you require, or alternatively to write the actual words on the candle.

To draw money towards you

**All cultures have their own ways of representing money
or luck, and this spell makes use of herbs and grasses
to draw money towards you. The coin should preferably
be new or rare, and therefore becomes a lucky token.
Initially, the paper money should also be new.**

YOU WILL NEED
- ✷ RED OR GREEN CHARM OR TALISMAN BAG
- ☽ SMALL COIN
- ● PAPER MONEY OF THE HIGHEST DENOMINATION YOU
  CAN AFFORD
- ◖ JOHN THE CONQUEROR ROOT
- ⚡ GOAT'S RUE ROOT (ALSO KNOWN AS DEVIL'S
  SHOESTRING), OR 9 ASH LEAVES
- ◗ PINE, OR SIMILAR INCENSE OR OIL FOR PROSPERITY

METHOD

Wrap the John the Conqueror root, small pieces of goat's
rue root or ash leaves and the coin in the paper money.

Ensure that you fold the money towards you.

Put everything into the charm bag.

Light the incense and hold the bag in the smoke.
Concentrate on the idea of gaining money.

Unobtrusively wear the bag when playing the lottery or
betting on horses. Alternatively, you might place it near
the door of your place of business to draw money to you.

You should find your finances show signs of improvement
within the next nine days.

 ● John the Conqueror root is considered to be one of
the most powerful herb roots available, so consider
your actions very carefully before deciding to use it. It is
believed that if someone else touches your lucky bag, the
good fortune is lost, so guard it carefully.

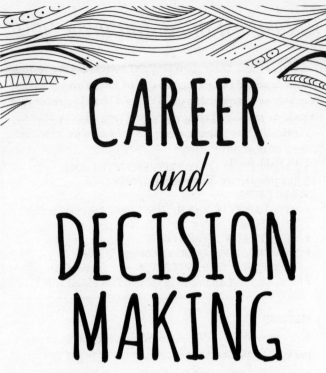

CAREER

and

DECISION MAKING

When thinking about your future in the workplace, mindfulness can really help you make the best of what you have and maximize your potential. Whether you're hoping to get a particular job or make an important business decision, the spells in this chapter can be used to bring success, improve communication skills and create new opportunities. There are also spells for helping study, removing obstacles and stopping office gossip.

Achieving a dream job

Candles always work well when dealing with aims and aspirations. This spell uses techniques involving the element of fire, which represents drive. This particular spell is best begun on the night of a New Moon.

YOU WILL NEED

- ✦ 2 BROWN CANDLES (TO REPRESENT THE JOB)
- ☽ GREEN CANDLE (FOR PROSPERITY)
- ● CANDLE TO REPRESENT YOURSELF (PERHAPS YOUR ASTROLOGICAL COLOUR)
- ◖ PROSPERITY INCENSE SUCH AS CINNAMON
- ⚡ PROSPERITY OIL SUCH AS BERGAMOT, OR BLENDED PATCHOULI AND BASIL

METHOD

Light your prosperity incense.

Anoint the candles with the prosperity oil from wick to end, since you want the good things to come towards you.

Place one of the brown candles in the centre of your chosen space.

Place the green one on the right, with your personal candle on the left.

(These candles should be in a safe place; they have to burn out entirely.)

As you light your personal candle, say:

 Open the way, clear my sight,

Bring me chance, that is my right.

Light the green candle, and say:

 Good luck is mine and true victory,

Help me Great Ones, come to me.

Light the brown candle, and say:

 Openings, work, rewards I see,
And as I will, so must it be.

Leave the candles to burn out completely.

Each night for a week – or until the candle is used up – light the second brown candle for 9 minutes while contemplating your dream job and the good to come out of it.

● You need to identify exactly what you mean by a 'dream job'. It is of little use aiming for something that is beyond your capabilities. You might apply for one initially, however, and this may begin to take you to where you want to be.

Success in finding a job

When you submit a job application, a manuscript for publication or anything requiring paper, there are several things that you can do using herbs, as well as some techniques based on ancient beliefs. One or all of the parts of the following techniques can be used, but first you must make your incense and dressing powder base.

FOR THE INCENSE AND DRESSING POWDER:

YOU WILL NEED
✦ 1 TEASPOON GROUND CINNAMON
☽ 1 TEASPOON GROUND GINGER
● 1 TEASPOON GROUND LEMON BALM
◗ FEW DROPS OF BERGAMOT OIL
⚡ BOWL

 METHOD
Mix all the ingredients together in the bowl.

To use as incense, leave it as it is, and burn it on a charcoal disc in a heatproof burner.

For the dressing powder, add a carrier such as powdered chalk or talcum powder, which should be unscented.

FOR THE SPELL PROPER:

 YOU WILL NEED
✦ YOUR PAPERS (APPLICATION FORM ETC)
⤵ ANY SUPPORTING DOCUMENTS (E.G. YOUR CV AND COVERING LETTER)

 METHOD

Light your incense.

Before you begin writing or filling in your forms, 'smoke' the paper on which you will write. This consists of wafting the required amount of paper or the application form in the incense smoke, and asking a blessing for the process you are about to start.

You may wish to place a crystal on your desk to help in the writing, or you could place it on or near your printer.

You might use tiger's eye for clearer thinking, or tourmaline to attract goodwill. Be guided by your own intuition.

Once you have completed the forms or the writing, you can 'dress' each page individually.

On the back of each page, sprinkle the dressing powder.

Draw your four fingers through the powder in wavy lines from top to bottom, so they leave very clear tracks.

Leave for a few moments, then shake off the powder, all the while visualizing the success of your project.

Finally, you can leave the papers in front of the image of your chosen deity, if you have one, or offer them for a blessing overnight.

• When you have completed this spell, you know that you have done as much as you can to ensure success. It is now in the hands of the gods. Obviously, you will already have done or will be doing any necessary research into your project on a physical level.

Now is the future that you promised yourself last year, last month, last week. Now is the only moment you'll ever really have. Mindfulness is about waking up to this.

Mark Williams

Resolving unfair treatment

A binding spell is performed by grasping the negative energy that is propelling a person or object, and stopping it. If you desire justice, which we often do, then call upon Egyptian goddess Maat, she who balances the scales. This spell might be used if you feel you are being unfairly treated by a colleague or a family member.

 YOU WILL NEED
- ✦ BLACK RIBBON, ABOUT 12 IN (30 CM) LONG
- ☽ WHITE FEATHER (TO REPRESENT MAAT)
- ● FRANKINCENSE INCENSE

 METHOD

Light the incense well before you take action, so that your sacred space is as clear as you can make it.

Contemplate your difficulty and acknowledge any part you may play in it.

Tie three knots in the ribbon – one in the middle, and one at each end.

As you tie the first knot, say:

Negativity here be bound.

As you tie the second knot, say:

Nastiness I do confound.

As you tie the third knot, say:

By power of three, I you impound.

Put the ribbon and the feather together on your altar or sacred space.

Leave it alone for three days for justice to be done.

After this time, take the ribbon and bury it, in open ground if possible.

Keep the feather in your drawer or purse as a reminder.

● You must remember to control your own emotions of hatred or fear, as you must be above reproach. When you feel that the problem has dissipated, be tolerant and try to remain on good terms with the person concerned, but never tell them what you have done.

 # To find the truth

One cannot make sensible decisions without the truth, and as one's intuition grows, it becomes easier to tell when people are not telling you the truth. This simple spell ensures that the truth is revealed in the right way.

 YOU WILL NEED
- ✦ HANDFUL OF THYME
- ☽ RED CANDLE
- ● FLAT DISH ON WHICH TO PUT THE HERBS

 METHOD
Pour the thyme into the dish, and say:

 Clarification I now require

So that truth is spoken

Let what is hidden now

Be brought into the open.

Light the candle, and say:

 Speak truth with passion

And goodbye to caution

As the truth is said

May I not be misled.

Allow the candle to burn down until the wax drips into the herbs.

Bury the cooled wax and herbs, preferably at a crossroads, having first blown the loose herbs to the wind.

• The herb thyme is said to bring courage, which is often needed to bypass our inhibitions. The colour red often represents sexual passion, but here it represents passion for the truth. Remember that sometimes the truth can hurt; a person may have been protecting you from it.

Consulting the oracle

For those who have developed intuition and learned to trust their foresightedness, this spell offers a way of having information come to you when it is needed. Do this during the waxing of (or at) the Full Moon. In her original form, the Greek goddess of justice Themis, on whom you will call in this spell, perceived everything in the past, the present and the future.

 YOU WILL NEED
✦ JASMINE OR LOTUS INCENSE
☽ YOUR PARTICULAR DIVINATION TOOLS (E.G. TAROT CARDS, RUNES AND A PENDULUM)
● CONTRACT OR PAPERS ON WHICH YOU NEED INFORMATION
◖ CHALICE CONTAINING RED WINE OR JUICE
⚡ 2 PURPLE CANDLES IN HOLDERS

METHOD
Light the incense.

Light the candles, placing one on each side of the chalice.

Place your divination tools and papers in between the candles, with the chalice above them.

Hold your hands over your divination tools or papers, and say:

 Goddess of Justice, Goddess of Law

Bless my working here today

Goddess of Honour, Goddess of Power

Show me the answer that I seek,

Through these tools I bid you speak.

Take three sips of the red wine or juice.

Do whatever you have to do with your tools – shuffle the cards and lay them out, lay out the runes, or ask your questions of the pendulum.

Sit quietly with the papers and reread them if necessary, knowing that the answer will come to you.

When you have finished, stand with your arms raised, and say:

 May the gods be thanked

May they aid me with their guidance.

The candles do not have to burn out, but can be used for another divinatory spell later.

• Because business decisions should not be made in a hurry, you will not necessarily receive all the information you need immediately, but you can expect to receive insights over a period of time. The spell can be re-activated very easily by holding your divinatory tools or the papers and repeating the last three lines of the invocation.

Open sesame

Sesame seeds are said to have the power to open locks, reveal hidden passages and find hidden treasures. They are also used in magic to induce lust. Here, however, they are used in a much more mundane way: to attract a good salary.

 YOU WILL NEED
- ✦ PRETTY GLASS OR CERAMIC BOWL
- ◗ HANDFUL OF SESAME SEEDS

 METHOD

Place the sesame seeds in the bowl.

Put the bowl somewhere near the door of your home in a safe space.

Each time you pass the bowl on your way out, give it a stir with your Apollo finger (ring finger) of your right hand.

Change the seeds every month, and dispose of them by burying them or throwing them into running water.

• When going for a job interview, try to ensure that you have some sesame oil. Decide what salary you want, then touch a little of the oil on the pulse spots on your wrists. Be confident in asking for the required sum.

Good fortune in business

This is a representational and herbal spell that uses a mirror as its vehicle. Mirrors have always been seen as mystical, and in this spell you are creating a doorway to riches. You could use paper money, but a coin is marginally better.

 YOU WILL NEED
* SMALL MIRROR
* POPPY SEEDS (FOR PROSPERITY)
* COIN OF THE HIGHEST DENOMINATION YOU CAN AFFORD
* PASTE GLUE

 METHOD

Paint the back of the mirror with the glue.

While it is still wet, sprinkle the poppy seeds on the glue.

Stick the coin in the centre of the back of the mirror.

Repeat three times:

Coin of the realm, seeds of plenty

May this business's coffers never be empty.

Hang the mirror on the back of the entrance door to the business.

• Perhaps the best way to think of the mirror in this spell is as a portal for money to flow through. The coin therefore acts as a focus for money energy. You should not use or allow the mirror to be used for grooming purposes. A square mirror suggests material manifestation, whereas a round mirror tends to enhance the energy.

🍶 Bay leaves wish spell

This spell uses plant magic and fire to achieve its purpose. The bay leaf possesses powerful magical properties for granting wishes. The first part of the spell is best done at the time of the New Moon, and the result will often have come to pass by the time of the Full Moon.

 YOU WILL NEED
- ✦ 3 BAY LEAVES
- ☽ PAPER OR PARCHMENT
- ● PEN
- 🕯 CANDLE

 METHOD

Write your wish three times on the paper, repeating it aloud.

Place the bay leaves on the paper.

Fold the paper into thirds and visualize your wish coming true.

Now fold the paper into thirds once again, and hide it away in a dark place.

Keep visualizing your wish coming true as you do this.

Once your wish is granted, burn the paper in the candle flame as a thank you, and allow the candle to burn out.

● This spell is best done in private, although it can also be performed on behalf of others. You should never reveal your wish to others, so be very sure that if the wish is for them, it is for the greater good. Bay leaves promote wisdom, thus protecting you from making mistakes.

Drawing out a latent talent

This charm is to bring out an existing talent and develop a potential – not to give you something you don't already have. If you have a secret ambition, you might try doing this spell. It uses herbs as its vehicle, and could be done at the time of the Crescent Moon.

YOU WILL NEED

- ✦ SMALL DRAWSTRING BAG, ABOUT 1–2 IN (2.5–5 CM) DEEP
- ☽ LIQUORICE ROOT POWDER
- ● ROSE HIPS
- ◖ FENNEL
- ⚡ CATNIP
- ◗ ELDERFLOWER

 METHOD

Put a pinch or two of the liquorice root, rose hips, fennel, catnip and elderflower in the bag.

Once assembled, hang the bag outdoors at sundown.

At midnight, remove the bag and place it around your neck.

If you like, you can make an affirmation before you sleep.

Say these words, or similar:

 As I sleep, I shall learn of my best potential.

You must then wear the charm bag for a full 24 hours to allow the spell to work.

After that time, you can place the charm bag under your pillow the night before anything important is to happen, whenever you feel you need some extra help in reaching your goals.

- Sleeping and dreaming are often the best ways we have of self-development. Most of us have secret ambitions but are prevented by doubts from succeeding. This spell helps to make those fears irrelevant.

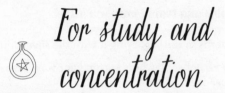

For study and concentration

It is sometimes important to go right back to basics to gain the help we need. This is a herbal and colour formula spell that calls on the powers of either Bridget, the goddess of poetry, or on Sarasvati, the Hindu goddess of knowledge. Your sachet should be purple for the former, or white for the latter.

 YOU WILL NEED
- 2 PARTS ROSEMARY
- 2 PARTS BASIL
- 1 PART CARAWAY SEEDS
- 1 PART DRIED RIND OF CITRUS FRUIT
- SMALL BOWL TO MIX THE HERBS
- SMALL CLOTH BAG
- SILVER THREAD OR CORD

 METHOD
Combine the herbs thoroughly while chanting one of the following.

For Bridget:

 Bridget, Brighde fashioner of words,

Help me now as I seek your aid,

Let me now bring you honour

In what I have to say today.

Or, for Sarasvati:

 Sarasvati, divine consort of Brahma,

Mistress of knowledge,

Teach me to use words wisely and well,

My doubts and fears I pray you dispel.

Put the herbs in the bag, tying it with the silver cord.

Place the sachet somewhere within your work area, where you can see it.

● You should discover that simply by focusing on the sachet you are able to free your mind from distractions and find inspiration as you study. If you become really stuck, pick up the sachet and allow some of the fragrance to escape, remembering to tie it back up when you have finished.

 # To help make a decision

This spell uses colour and candles to allow you to make a decision between two opposing outcomes. You are in a sense taking the dilemma to the highest authority in order for the best outcome to become apparent. Do the spell at the time of the New Moon if there is a new beginning involved.

YOU WILL NEED
✦ 2 YELLOW CANDLES
☽ WHITE CANDLE OR YOUR ASTROLOGICAL CANDLE
● LENGTH OF PURPLE RIBBON, ABOUT 2 FT (60 CM) LONG
◗ 2 PIECES OF PAPER
⚡ PEN

 METHOD
This spell takes three days to do in total.

Place the white candle on the exact middle of the ribbon.

The ribbon signifies the highest possible spiritually correct energy.

Place the two yellow candles at either end of the ribbon.

Write the two possible outcomes on the pieces of paper and fold them separately.

Place these two papers under the yellow candles on top of the ribbon.

Light the middle (white) candle first, and then the two outer (yellow) ones.

Acknowledge the fact that you will be extinguishing them as part of the spell.

Burn the candles for at least an hour, so that a link is properly made.

Consider both decisions carefully.

Snuff the candles out.

The next day, move the papers and the outer candles closer to the middle candle.

Roll the ribbon in towards the centre against the candle bases.

Relight the candles and again burn for at least an hour.

Repeat each day until all the candles are grouped together. (This should take at least three days, and, if time allows, longer.) Ensure that you have at least an hour's burning time left for the final day.

Allow the candles to burn out, and within three days you should find it easy to make a decision.

• This process allows due consideration of all the pros and cons of the various options. It provides the energy for the correct decision and allows you to be rational and objective while still taking account of the emotional aspects. The method keeps your mind focused on the matter at hand. You do not then 'stand in your own light', that is, get in the way of your own success.

 # Legal success

This spell is based on ancient herb and folk magic. To influence the outcome of legal procedures, the associated papers are 'dressed' to give added power to any decisions that have to be made. The technique is very simple and, of course, can also be used in business proceedings, but in this case it should probably be carried out away from the office.

 YOU WILL NEED
- ✦ YOUR DOCUMENTS
- ⟡ DRESSING POWDER, CONSISTING OF:
  - ● UNSCENTED TALCUM OR POWDERED CHALK
  - ◖ DEER'S TONGUE LEAVES
  - ⚡ CALENDULA FLOWERS
  - ◗ GINGER OR CINNAMON POWDER

 METHOD

Combine the leaves, flowers and ginger or cinnamon powder in equal measures with the talcum or chalk.

Place your documents on a flat surface and sprinkle them thoroughly with the mixture.

Draw your fingernails through the powder in wavy lines from top to bottom.

As you do so, concentrate on the desired outcome.

Leave the papers overnight, then shake off the powder in the morning.

● This spell does not seem to work if there is any dishonesty or deliberate nefarious dealings on your part. If you are completely above board, however, it is possible to turn things in your favour. The method of 'dressing' papers can also be carried out if you have important exams or studying to do.

Mindful leadership keeps you cool and energetic in any situation, so that you can make the best possible decisions.

Amit Ray

Good communication

The crystal carnelian can be used in business spells when you want to be heard. It is an excellent stone to wear or carry for public speaking, as it strengthens the voice and confers eloquence on the speaker. It can also be used to counteract doubt and negative thoughts, and it is used for that purpose in this spell.

 YOU WILL NEED
- SMALL PIECE OF CARNELIAN
- INCENSE SUCH AS BENZOIN WHICH IS SACRED TO MERCURY, THE ROMAN GOD OF COMMUNICATION

 METHOD

The night before an important meeting, light your incense.

Hold the carnelian in the smoke of the incense, and say:

Mercury, Ogmios, Heracles,

    Gods of eloquence and right speech,

    Help me tomorrow to say the right thing

    To make myself heard.

Then sleep with the carnelian under your pillow, since one of its properties is to prevent nightmares.

On the day of the meeting, either have the piece of carnelian discreetly in front of you where you can see it, or keep it in your pocket where you can easily reach it.

When stuck for words or in difficulty, either touch the stone or mentally make a link with it. This will enable you to overcome the blockage.

● Simply having something else to focus on is good anyway, but having appealed to the gods, you draw on the very source of communication and on the qualities of the crystal. Afterwards, remember to thank the three gods.

Winning a deal

This spell uses candle magic, as well as representational and colour magic. It is probably best done at the time of the Full Moon if the deal is a merger or acquisition, or the New Moon if it initiates new projects or implements new ideas. Thursday is also a good day, being one to maximize opportunities. Because you are using woods and plants in the incense, the method will create a fair amount of smoke, so it is better to do it away from the office, unless you can be undisturbed.

YOU WILL NEED

- ✱ FOR SUCCESS INSENCE:
  - ☽ 1 PART EACH OF BASIL, BAY AND OAK
  - ● 2 PARTS CEDARWOOD
- ◍ BOWL TO MIX INCENSE
- ⚡ WHITE CANDLE
- ◗ YOUR BURIN OR A PIN
- ❰ YOUR COPY OF THE PAPERS NECESSARY FOR THE SUCCESSFUL DEAL

METHOD

While you mix your incense, bear in mind the outcome you require.

You might appeal to Thor at the same time, or to Ganesha, another god of opportunity.

Inscribe your candle with either a sign for money, or the Ehwaz, the rune for success in partnership, which is:

Light your candle and the incense.

Sit for a few moments, then hold the legal papers in the smoke of the incense.

Visualize the required outcome such as signing the papers.

While the candle is burning out, reinforce your vision of success.

● Any outcome that occurs because of this spell is not time-specific, i.e. you have not asked for a particular time frame. If a deadline is required, you should use 'Fast luck oil' (pages 130–1) to anoint your candle before you inscribe it.

To remove obstacles

In this spell, Ganesha the elephant-headed Hindu god is invoked to ensure the success of any difficult task and to grant wishes. Because he represents a combination of strength and shrewdness, he is able to get rid of the most intimidating of barriers. We have categorized this as a career spell, although obviously it can be adjusted to encompass other life decisions too.

YOU WILL NEED:
- ✦ YELLOW CANDLE
- ☽ RED CANDLE
- ● YOUR FAVOURITE FLOWERS
- ◖ SANDALWOOD POWDER
- ⚡ FIGURE OF GANESHA OR AN ELEPHANT
- ◗ COOKED RICE
- ◖ PEN AND PAPER

 METHOD

Place the flowers and rice in front of the figure while the sandalwood is burning.

With your fingertips to your forehead and your hands together, bow to the statue, and say:

Greetings, Ganesha,

Welcome to my sacred space

With your help, all success shall be mine.

I come to you, knowing you will grant my wishes

All impediments are removed.

I honour your presence,

Good fortune be with you and with me and mine.

I praise you Ganesha!

Light the yellow and red candles, and tell Ganesha what you most desire.

Now commit your wishes to paper, and place the paper under the statue.

Say:

 God of wisdom, God of strength

Loving bringer of success

Take now these wishes of mine

Mould them, shape them, work them

Till together we can bring them to fruition.

Bow as before, then put the candles out.

Repeat for the following two days, finally letting the candles burn themselves out.

Afterwards, do not disturb the statue for three days, and never ask for the same thing twice.

• Before long, often within three days, a new way will be shown to enable you to achieve your objective. Remember to give thanks by sharing your good fortune with others and making a further offering to Ganesha, who appreciates the effort you have made.

To improve your boss's attitude

This combination of a candle and mirror spell is designed to improve your work environment. It is equally appropriate for all levels of work relationships. Often a spell relating to work is best done at home and a reminder taken into the workplace to reinforce it. The spell is carried out for seven days and then reinforced once a week. Tuesdays or Thursdays are good days to try.

YOU WILL NEED

- ✦ SMALL MIRROR THAT WILL FIT UNOBTRUSIVELY IN YOUR DRAWER
- ☽ WHITE CANDLE
- ● OIL SUCH AS JASMINE FOR SPIRITUAL LOVE, OR YLANG YLANG FOR BALANCE

METHOD

Anoint the candle.

Light the candle and burn it for at least an hour.

Concentrate for a few minutes on the image of your boss as they are when they annoy you.

Look in the mirror and visualize your boss being pleasant and calm.

See yourself working with them as an efficient team.

Carry on doing this each evening for a week, then do it once a week thereafter for at least six weeks.

In between times, keep the mirror in your desk drawer and reinforce the visualization of your boss being calm every day.

● You should see an improvement after a week, and others may also notice a change as time goes by. As you become less stressed, you may find that you become more creative and can deal better with other petty annoyances.

Knot spell

**To rid yourself of problems or a troublesome situation,
you can use a representation of the difficulty in a tangled
and knotted length of yarn. There are then differing ways
of getting rid of the problem. This spell is best done at the
time of the Full Moon, and is in two parts.**

 YOU WILL NEED
- ✶ BIODEGRADABLE STRING OR COTTON YARN
- ☽ INGREDIENTS FOR A RITUAL BATH (INCLUDING
  CANDLES AND A PURIFICATION OIL)

 METHOD – PART ONE

Your string or yarn needs to be biodegradable, because this
reinforces the idea that your problems will dissolve. It can
be in the appropriate colour for the problem to be solved
(e.g. green for money, red for love etc).

Sit quietly and think of all your fears and problems. Let
them pass into the string.

Tie the string in knots to symbolize how confused your
problems make you feel.

One way of dealing with your difficulties is to take the
knotted string to a high place and let the wind blow it
away, along with your negativity.

A second way is to bury the string in soft ground, although
this method will mean that the resolution of your
problems may come slowly.

A third way is to begin to untie the knots, and as you do
so, ask for help in seeing solutions. This does not have to
be done all at once; it can be done over time.

 METHOD – PART TWO

Whichever method you use, make sure you take a ritual
bath or shower to cleanse yourself after working with
the string.

You need three candles: one to represent yourself, a black one to signify negativity, and another one in the colour of your choice to suggest your life without problems.

Anoint the candles with a purification or blessing oil.

Anoint the black candle from the end to the wick, to remove bad luck. Anoint the other candles from the wick to the end, to bring you what you desire.

Have your ritual bath as usual.

● This spell has two parts, first getting rid of your problems, then cleansing yourself of the effects. Only then can you decide how you are going to make changes in your life so that you do not attract yet more problems.

 # *Encourage risk taking*

This spell uses candles and the Ogham Staves, an ancient symbolic alphabet that is similar to the runes and was used by the Celtic people. Today, we tend to use the representations singly in the form of amulets, or as here to inscribe candles. In addition, we can also use herb oils for courage.

 YOU WILL NEED
✦ WHITE CANDLE
⟩ ST JOHN'S WORT OIL OR SAGE
● YOUR BURIN

METHOD

Anoint your candle with the oil (for courage).

Inscribe it with the Ogham Stave Coll, which represents wisdom:

Light the candle.

Ask for help from the Irish God Ogma, who gave us the staves, in whatever task you are about to undertake.

As the candle burns, think about what the risks might be in your venture, and what you can do to minimize them.

● This spell is designed to give you the courage and wisdom to take risks in whatever way is appropriate for you. It need not be a business risk, but some way in which you must stretch your own boundaries. It does not ensure success, but allows you the potential for achievement.

 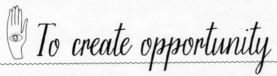

This spell appeals to the Roman goddess Ops, who used to be petitioned by sitting down and touching the earth with one hand, since she was a deity of prosperity, crops and fertility. Using sympathetic magic during the Full Moon, a wish doll (poppet) representing health and happiness is made to draw opportunities towards you.

 YOU WILL NEED
✦ BOWL OF SAND (TO REPRESENT EARTH)
☽ GREEN CLOTH
● NEEDLE AND THREAD
◗ PEN
⚡ CINNAMON OR CEDAR INCENSE
◗ DRIED CHAMOMILE, VERVAIN OR SQUILL
◖ MINT AND HONEYSUCKLE OIL

METHOD
Make a poppet out of the cloth (see pages 29–30).

Add a few drops of the oils to the dried herbs.

While concentrating on the opportunities available to you or your business, write your name on the poppet and stuff it with the oil-infused herbs.

Sew the figure shut.

Light the incense.

Hold the poppet in the incense smoke, and say:

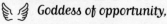 *Goddess of opportunity,*

Bring good fortune now to me

Guide me by your gentle hand

For I am as worthy as these grains of sand.

Let the sand trickle through your fingers to signify touching the earth.

Repeat this an odd number of times (seven works very well).

Keep your poppet safe. You don't have to have it with you at all times, but just with your possessions or papers. For the spell to continue to work, renew it every Full Moon.

● This is a good spell to use for business opportunities, since the poppet can be kept unobtrusively in a drawer or cupboard, and hopefully will become imbued with the excitement of your day-to-day work. It can also be used when you wish to enhance your career prospects.

Each morning we're born again,
of yesterday nothing remains,
what's left began today.

Anselm Hollo

Weaving success

This knot spell is an unobtrusive way of enhancing the energy of your business, as well as ensuring its security. Braiding three strands links us with the triple-aspected Great Mother: Maid, Mother, Crone.

YOU WILL NEED
- ✦ 3 EQUAL LENGTHS OF RIBBON:
  - ❯ DARK BLUE FOR SUCCESS IN LONG-TERM PLANS, AND CLARITY
  - ● YELLOW FOR MENTAL POWER, WEALTH, COMMUNICATION AND TRAVEL
  - ◗ BROWN FOR GROUNDING, STABILITY AND ENDURANCE
- ⚡ LARGE SAFETY PIN

METHOD

Pin the three ribbons together at the top to make braiding easier. Braid them together neatly.

As you do so, repeat the following words as often as you feel is right, remembering the significances of the colours:

 Great Mother, Great Mother

Come to me now

As these strands weave and become one

May this business grow.

Now loop the braid around the front door handle, so that anyone who comes into the business must go past it.

● You should find that the qualities you have woven into the business begin to bring results very quickly. Combinations of different colours will have different results: red will bring vitality and willpower; orange will bring success and prosperity through creativity; and yellow will bring communication, mental power and wealth.

Stop gossip

This spell utilizes representational magic, and is a way to stop malicious gossip. It is useful in an office environment where factions almost inevitably arise and people become embroiled. All that is necessary is to identify the ring leader.

 YOU WILL NEED
- ✶ SAMPLE OF THE PERSON'S HANDWRITING (FAILING THAT, A PIECE OF PAPER THAT HAS BEEN HANDLED BY THEM)
- ☽ JAR WITH A SCREW-TOP LID
- ● WAX, TO SEAL THE JAR

 METHOD

Place the sample of handwriting or paper in the jar and screw it tightly shut.

Carry this away from the offending person.

If the badmouthing does not stop immediately, take the jar and seal it with the wax, saying:

 Gossip and ill-feeling begone

Trouble us no more.

This should have the desired effect.

When the difficulty has clearly passed, remove the paper from the jar and burn it.

Do not use the jar again for magical purposes.

● With this spell, remember that you are not binding the person, you are stopping their specific action, so releasing the paper means you are indicating that you are no longer involved with them. The person must be free to go their own way. Also try to make sure that you do not get involved in other people's gossip.

Ceridwen's spell

This spell pays homage to the Welsh goddess Ceridwen, who was the nurturer of a druidic bard known as Taliesin. Ceridwen is invoked here and asked for the gift of inspiration, called Awen by the druids. This brings poetic inspiration, prophecy and the ability to shape-shift (become something else). In bringing about change, this becomes a spell for creativity in all its forms. One of Ceridwen's symbols is the cauldron.

YOU WILL NEED
- CAULDRON
- SEEDS (PREFERABLY WHEAT)
- WHITE CANDLE
- INCENSE MADE UP OF:
  - 1 PART ROSEBUDS
  - 1 PART CEDARWOOD CHIPS
  - 1 PART SWEET MYRRH

METHOD

Blend your incense the night before you plan to use it.

Light your incense and the candle.

Place the cauldron in front of you and half-fill it with wheat seeds. Stir the cauldron clockwise three times, and let the seeds trickle through your fingers as you say:

 Ceridwen, Ceridwen,

I seek your favour

Just as you searched for the boy Gwion

So I search for the power of Awen

Inspiration to be what I must, to discover the known,

And to flow with change.

Grant, I pray, this power.

Since Awen is a threefold gift, you should repeat the stirring of the cauldron twice more, or once on each of the next two days.

When you have finished, tip the remains of the incense into the cauldron and bury the contents.

The candle may be snuffed out, but do not use it for anything else.

• Ceridwen is said to have brewed herbs together to bring the gift of inspiration to her ugly son Agfaddu. Gwion was supposed to guard the potion but, in being splashed by it, absorbed its powers. In escaping the wrath of Ceridwen, Gwion became a seed of corn and was swallowed by her in the guise of a black hen. The Welsh bard Taliesin, born nine months later, was thus an initiated form of the boy. Artists, writers and poets can all seek this kind of inspiration.

 Luck in business

This herbal charm bag can be further enhanced by adding new coins to represent money. Comfrey protects the owner while travelling, and dragon's blood adds zing. The technique is best done at the time of the Waxing Moon, on a Wednesday or a Thursday.

YOU WILL NEED
- ✴ DRAWSTRING BAG, ABOUT 2–4 IN (5–10 CM) DEEP
- ☽ BAYBERRY
- ● RED CLOVER
- ◗ COMFREY
- ⚡ DRAGON'S BLOOD
- ◗ MANDRAKE ROOT
- ◖ 5–6 TULIP PETALS
- ♥ 3 NEW COINS, IF WANTED

 METHOD
Put equal measures of the herbs into the bag.

Inscribe your full name on one side of the mandrake root, then inscribe the following runes on the other side.

Dagaz (for clear vision and awareness):

Fehu (for wealth):

Teiwaz (for justice and altruism):

Put the mandrake root into the bag along with the coins, if you use them.

Consecrate and charge the bag.

Keep it in your pocket, in the cash box or on a windowsill, remembering to shake it occasionally to activate the energy.

● This charm works very well if you are in business for yourself. When inscribing the mandrake, you can use your business name or logo, if you wish. If you can make it a regular routine to reinforce its aims every week, you should not have any problems.

Moon wishes

This spell harnesses the Moon's energy, and can be done at both the New and Full Moon. By meditating before you sleep, you allow influences from your higher self – the part that knows what is right for you – to come through.

 YOU WILL NEED
- ✦ 5 WHITE CANDLES
- ☽ COLOURED CANDLE OF YOUR CHOICE (PERHAPS REPRESENTING A WISH, OR IN THE COLOUR OF YOUR ASTROLOGICAL SIGN)

METHOD

Clear your mind of all clutter, or meditate for a short time to be sure you have clarified your wishes.

Place the white candles in the shape of a pentagram where they can burn safely:

Light the five candles, starting from the top first and working clockwise. Or, if it feels right, light them according to the connecting lines of the pentagram, again starting at the top. As you do so, say:

 Moon above which glows so bright

Guard my sleep so deep tonight

I pray to you with this request

My life works out at my behest.

Allow the candles to burn for at least half an hour before putting them out and composing yourself for sleep.

The next morning, light the other candle and meditate or contemplate your wishes for another 30 minutes.

Spend some time visualizing what life will be like when your wishes are granted.

Repeat this whole procedure for the next three nights.

Finally, on the fourth morning, relight all of the candles and allow them to burn out while you play some rousing music that means something to you.

In the last hour, while the candles are still burning, reconsider your wishes and make any adjustments to them that seem realistic.

• This spell takes some time to complete, and also requires that you spend a fair amount of time in contemplation. It does mean, however, that you can be realistic in your expectations, and there should be few blocks to achieving what you want. There is no need to be frivolous.

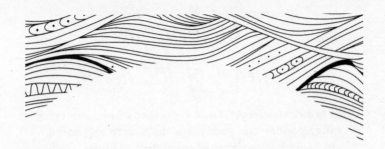

PROTECTION

Using mindful spells to protect our own personal space as well as those around us creates a cleansing feeling of calm while banishing negative energies. If we ever feel threatened or are worried about the safety of our children, the spells in this chapter will help to invoke feelings of safety, shelter and defence from potential negativity and harm, giving us a visual image of security to carry with us wherever we go. Spells include protecting a child, travelling safely, breaking a curse and protecting a pet. There are also suggestions for a variety of amulets you might use, such as anchors, bells, keys, knots, pine cones and seashells.

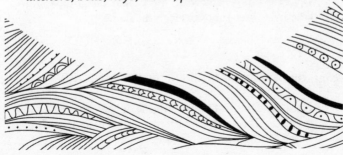

A blessing for the heart of the home

This is a candle, crystal and representational spell that calls upon Hestia, goddess of the hearth and home, to bring her qualities of constancy, calmness and gentleness to bear on your home. Hestia is supportive of the family, and home and was praised by the poet Homer in ancient Greece.

 YOU WILL NEED
- LAVENDER CANDLE
- SMALL SILVER OR BRASS BOWL IN WHICH TO STAND THE CANDLE
- LAVENDER FLOWERS
- SMALL PIECE OF AMETHYST

 METHOD

Raise the empty bowl above your head in both hands, and say:

Hestia, you who tends the holy house of the lord Apollo,

Draw near, and bestow grace upon my home.

Place the candle in the bowl, making certain the candle will stand firmly.

Light the candle, and when it is properly alight, pass the amethyst three times through the flame.

Say:

Hestia, glorious is your portion and your right.

Place the amethyst in your hearth or close to your fireplace. (If you have no fireplace, then place it as close to the centre of your home as possible.)

Sprinkle some of the lavender flowers across your doorway to keep your home safe.

Say:

 Hail Hestia, I will remember you.

Allow the candle to burn down, then place some of the lavender flowers in the bowl, leaving it in a safe space.

• At times when the atmosphere in the home becomes somewhat fraught, this spell can bring a period of peace and tranquillity. The bowl, lavender flowers and amethyst are all sacred to Hestia, and remind you of her presence.

 # To guard against road rage

One aspect of protective devices is to make them appropriate for the circumstances in which we find ourselves. For protection against our own or someone else's road rage, we can use a sachet of herbs together with representational objects, then fashion a charm bag that is reactivated for its purpose on each journey.

 YOU WILL NEED
- ✦ PIECE OF COMFREY ROOT
- ☽ 2 BAY LEAVES
- • ST CHRISTOPHER MEDAL, OR RUNE OF ELHAZ INSCRIBED ON PAPER
- ◖ SMALL PIECE OF ROSE QUARTZ
- ⚡ ROSE-PINK OR GREEN SACHET

 METHOD

As you fill your sachet or charm bag with the items, bear in mind the purpose of each object:

Comfrey root is for protection. Bay leaves drive away negativity. St Christopher is for travellers, or the rune is to remind you of your responsibilities. Rose quartz brings about healing and loving feelings.

All the ingredients together represent your ability to be in harmony with the rest of the world.

Place the sachet in the glove compartment of your car, or hang it from the rear-view mirror where it cannot obscure your view.

When you find yourself getting irritated or faced by someone else's irritation, simply look at, touch or hold the sachet.

● Each time you travel, remember that this particular device works specifically against road rage, so it needs to be held briefly beforehand to guard against unforeseen incidents. Hopefully you will then set out on your journey in a calm and relaxed state of mind.

To summon help from the elements

This technique is an excellent example of how you can ask the elements for assistance. You use representations of each element, then address the spirits of each one in turn to seek their help. When you have finished your task, each element is then honoured by returning it to the earth.

 YOU WILL NEED
✦ WHITE CANDLE (TO REPRESENT FIRE)
☾ SMALL BOWL OF SALT OR SAND (TO REPRESENT EARTH)
● SMALL BOWL OF WATER
◗ INCENSE SUCH AS BERGAMOT (TO REPRESENT AIR)

METHOD
Light the incense and the candle.

As you do this, bear in mind that at this stage you are making use of the elements of fire and air.

Call upon the power of these elements.

Ask for their help in the work you are about to do.

Preferably use your own words, but keep them simple.

For fire, you might say something like:

I request your presence, Oh Spirit of Fire
I ask for your help, your power I require.

For air, your words might be:

Come to me now, Oh Spirit of Air
I pray above all for a mind that is clear.

Lift the bowl of salt and likewise invoke the powers of the earth element.

Say perhaps:

Approach now I pray, Oh Spirit of Earth
Help I do need, and prove now my worth.

Do the same with the water.

Say:

Come to me now, Oh Spirit of Water
My feelings are clear, your strength is now sought for.

When you have finished, sprinkle the salt or sand on the earth, pour the water onto the earth, bury the ashes of the incense and snuff out the candle.

● This is not really a spell as such, but more a preparation for magical working. It allows you to set up a sacred space very quickly. From there, you can cast a protective circle within which to carry out your more important workings.

Cleansing the body of negative energies

This ritual is a protection spell using candle magic and an appeal to the elements. One aspect needs to be noted: black candles were once associated with Black Magic and malevolence, but today they are much more commonly used to represent loss, sadness, discord and negativity.

 YOU WILL NEED
- ✦ WHITE CANDLE (FOR POSITIVE ENERGY)
- ☽ BLACK OR DARK BLUE CANDLE (FOR NEGATIVE ENERGY)
- ● GREEN CANDLE (FOR HEALING)

 METHOD

In your sacred space, place the candles in a triangle, with the green candle closest to you. Clear your mind of everything except what you are doing.

Light the white candle, being aware of its symbolism, and say the following:

 Earth, Fire, Wind, Water and Spirit,

   I ask thee to cleanse my body of all negative energies.

Light the black or blue candle, also being aware of its symbolism.

Repeat the words above, then pause to let the energies come to a natural balance.

Light the green candle, and again repeat the above words.

Sit back, keep your mind clear and be peaceful for at least 10 minutes.

When the time feels right, either snuff out the candles or allow the green one to burn right down so that you are filled with healing energy.

- You should feel rested and relaxed, and more ready to tackle problems as they arise. Make this part of your weekly routine until you feel it is no longer necessary.

When you feel threatened

We all go through times when we feel that we are under threat – perhaps at work when schedules are tight and tempers are about to snap, or maybe in the home when tensions are making themselves felt, creating a chill in the air. This spell, which calls for excellent visualization skills, protects you by forming a crystal shell around you, keeping you shielded from the bad vibrations of ill temper.

YOU WILL NEED
- CLEAR CRYSTAL OF QUARTZ, OR ANY FAVOURITE CRYSTAL THAT IS FULL OF CLEAR LIGHT

METHOD

Place the crystal where it will catch the sunshine.

Sit near it and breathe in deeply through your nose.

Hold your breath for a moment or two before exhaling through your mouth.

Repeat this several times, absorbing the light cast by the crystal as you inhale, then exhaling any negative feelings, doubts and darkness.

After a minute or two, stand up and begin visualizing a crystal-like ring rising around you, from your feet upwards, getting higher and higher with each breath you take.

When the crystal ring is above head height, see it close over you, forming any shape in which you feel comfortable to be enclosed – a pyramid perhaps, or maybe a dome.

Still breathing deeply, feel the 'crystal' form a floor beneath your feet.

Conversely, sense a link between you and the centre of the Earth.

Stretch your arms and feel your fingers touch the sides of your 'crystal'.

Look upwards and see the top of the pyramid point or dome.

If you can, also try to view yourself from outside the protective 'crystal' in which you have surrounded yourself.

Now say:

Within this crystal, I am safe from negative thought,

And am so wherever I might be.

When you feel it is right to do so, return to normal breathing and see the 'crystal' open to allow you to step outside it or perceive it dissolving.

This visualization can be used wherever you are, perhaps in a crowd, a sticky situation or simply under pressure, safe in the knowledge that you can return to it whenever you need to.

• Those who have used this spell find that keeping a crystal in the house, office, or wherever else they think they may need protection from negativity strengthens the spell's potency. 'To protect a child' (pages 201–2) is a similar sort of spell, and if the idea of being inside a crystal seems strange, you could start off with the method from that spell instead.

Fire protection spell

This spell uses the element of fire to protect you, creating a visual image that you carry throughout your daily life. It requires a clear space outdoors of about 20 ft (6 m) in diameter initially, and you must be careful not to set any vegetation alight through the heat of your fires. You can also perform this spell on a beach, if fires are permitted.

YOU WILL NEED
* ✦ ENOUGH FALLEN WOOD TO FEED FOUR FIRES
* ☽ DRY BRUSHWOOD OR PAPER, TO START THE FIRES
* ● MATCHES
* ◗ WATER, TO DOUSE THE FIRE

METHOD

You should make sure that you only gather fallen wood or driftwood.

Make sure you have enough to keep each of the fires burning for about half an hour.

Taking up one of the sticks of wood, draw a rough circle about 11 ft (3.3 m) in diameter. Determine the four directions: north, east, south and west (use a compass, the Sun, Moon or stars).

Lay a small fire at each point just inside the circle, but do not light them.

Put spare wood safely beside each fire to keep them burning for at least half an hour.

Walking to the south first, light the fire, proclaiming as you do:

 Nothing from the South can harm me
Welcome Spirits of the South.

Wait until one of the pieces of wood is burning, pick it up and move to the west.

Light the fire, and say:

Nothing from the West can harm me
Welcome Spirits of the West.

Again, take up a burning branch and move to the north.

Light the fire while saying:

Nothing from the North can harm me
Welcome Spirits of the North.

Again, take up a burning piece of wood and take it to the east.

Light that fire and say:

Nothing from the East can harm me
Welcome Spirits of the East.

Next, take up a burning branch and carry it back to the south.

Thrust it into the southern fire and choose a new branch.

Use the new branch to trace an arc above your head from south to north, saying:

Nothing from Above can harm me
Welcome Spirits from Above.

Finally, throw the wood down in the centre of the circle and say:

Nothing from Below can harm me
Let Spirits come who wish me well.

This last stick represents Aether or spirit, and the technique creates a sphere of energy that you can call on whenever you need it.

You can replace that piece of wood into the southern fire if you wish, or contemplate it as it burns out.

Replenish the fires as necessary.

Sit in the centre of the circle and recognise that the fires are purifying and cleansing your personal environment on every level of existence.

Watch each fire carefully to see if you can perceive the spirits of the elements:

- ✦ Salamanders for fire.
- ☾ Gnomes, dryads or brownies for earth.
- ● Sylphs for air.
- ◗ Undines for water.

Revel in the warmth of the fires, appreciate their light and sense their protection.

Remember these feelings, as they are what will protect you as you leave the space.

When the fires begin to die down, douse them with the water and bury the embers to prevent them flaring again.

Erase the markings of the circle and leave the space.

● This spell or ritual (depending on how ornate you wish to make it) is done in the open air to create a barrier of protection for you, but it may also make you more conscious of how fire works. In this case, it consumes that which is dead and finished with, leaving only its power in its wake.

Change the future by changing the present. Don't wait to start. Start now.

Akiroq Brost

To reverse negativity or hexes

Try this candle spell using the element of fire to reverse any negativity or hexes being sent in your direction. Anger from others can often be dealt with in this way, but deliberate maliciousness may require more force. You need to be as dispassionate as you can when dealing with a hex, which is defined as 'an evil spell'.

YOU WILL NEED
- ✦ PURPLE CANDLE
- ☽ ROSEMARY OIL
- ● WHITE PAPER
- ◗ BLACK INK
- ⚡ FIREPROOF DISH SUCH AS YOUR CAULDRON OR AN ASHTRAY

METHOD

Visualize all blocks in your life path being removed.

Anoint your candle with the oil.

On the piece of paper, write in black ink:

 All blocks are now removed.

Fold the paper three times away from you. Light the candle and burn the paper in your dish.

Invoke the power of fire and its elemental spirits by repeating three times:

 Firedrakes and salamanders,

Aid me in my quest,

Protect me from all evil thoughts

Turn away and send back this hex.

After the third repetition, close the spell in whatever way is appropriate for you.

A simple statement is enough:

 Let it be so.

• No one has the right to curse or malign another person, and all you are doing with this spell is turning the negativity back where it belongs. When you use the power of fire, you are harnessing one of the most potent forces of the universe, so be sure you use it wisely and well.

 # Welcoming household gods

Deities relating to the home are found in most folk religions. In Rome, the 'penates' were household gods who were worshipped in connection with the 'lares' (beneficent spirits of ancestors) and, as guardians of the hearth, with Vesta or Hestia. This spell is representational and pays due deference to them for protection from harm.

YOU WILL NEED
- ✴ REPRESENTATION OF YOUR HOUSEHOLD GODS (A STATUE, PICTURE OR SOMETHING SIGNIFICANT FOR YOU)
- ☽ REPRESENTATIONS OF YOUR ANCESTORS (PERHAPS A GIFT FROM A GRANDPARENT, AN HEIRLOOM OR A PHOTOGRAPH)
- • FRESH FLOWERS OR TAPER CANDLES
- ◊ INCENSE STICKS OF YOUR CHOICE
- ⚡ BOWL OF UNCOOKED RICE
- ◗ BOWL OF WATER

 METHOD
This technique offers food to the gods and the ancestors, and blends pagan and Western thought.

Place your representational objects either close to your kitchen door or near the cooker (today often considered the heart of the home).

Light your incense and place the bowls in position in front.

Light the candles or place the flowers so that you have created a shrine.

Spend a little time communing with the penates and lares. Welcome them into your home and give thanks for their help and protection.

(In Thailand, a quite intricate 'spirit house' is provided away from the shadow of the house for the ancestors.)

Their presence is acknowledged each day so that they do not become restless.

Replace the water and rice weekly.

• Remembering to honour the household gods and the ancestors means that their spirits will look favourably upon us at all times. Whenever there is a problem, often taking it to the household gods for consideration is enough to have the resolution become apparent.

Invoking the household gods

This ritual is best performed during the Waxing Moon. It could be considered a kind of birthday party, so feel free to include food and drink as part of it, if you wish.

YOU WILL NEED
- ✦ INCENSE THAT REMINDS YOU OF HERBS, FORESTS AND GREEN GROWING THINGS
- ☽ GREEN CANDLE IN A HOLDER
- ● YOUR WAND
- ◖ SMALL STATUES OF DEER OR OTHER FOREST ANIMALS
- ◗ PINE CONES, IVY AND HOLLY, OR SOMETHING SIMILAR
- ◖ SYMBOL APPROPRIATE TO YOUR GUARDIAN (E.G. CRESCENT MOON FOR THE MOON GODDESS)

METHOD

Decorate the area around the symbol of your guardian with the greenery.

Clean the guardian symbol so that there is no dust or dirt on it.

If the symbol is small enough, put it on the altar, otherwise leave it nearby.

Light the incense and candle.

Stand before your altar, and say:

Guardian spirits, I invite you to join me at this altar. You are my friends and I wish to thank you.

Take the incense and circle the guardian symbol three times, moving clockwise while saying:

Thank you for the help you give to keep this home clean and pleasant.

Move the candle clockwise around the symbol three times, and say:

Thank you for the light you send to purify this space and dispel the darkness.

With the wand in the hand you consider most powerful, encircle the symbol again three times clockwise, and say:

I now ask for your help and protection for me, my family and all who live herein.

I ask that you remove all trouble makers of all sorts, incarnate and discarnate.

I thank you for your love and understanding.

Stand with your arms raised up.

Call upon your own deity, and say:

 [Name of deity] I now invoke the guardian of this household whom I have invited into my home.

I honour it in this symbol of its being.

I ask a blessing and I add my thanks for its protection and friendship.

• If you have more than one guardian, change all instances of 'it' to 'their', and so on. Spend a few moments lovingly caressing the symbol, sending out the thought that the guardian is important to you. Be aware of the subtle changes in atmosphere that occur as the protective spirits become part of your environment. Finally, thank the unseen participants.

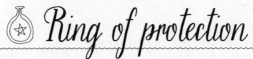

Ring of protection

In this method of working, you place a protective shield of light around your home so that no harm can come to either it or the people therein.

 YOU WILL NEED
✦ THE POWER OF YOUR OWN MIND

 METHOD

Visualize a ring of light surrounding your property.

Ask your guardians or favourite deities to protect your home and its occupants for as long as necessary.

Reinforce the circle of light whenever you go away or, indeed, whenever you think about it.

It really is that simple!

• Once you become adept at visualizing a ring of light, this spell can be done quickly and easily, as often as you like. The light acts as a bubble or shield to protect your home.

Keep your child safe

This technique is based on an old nursery rhyme which began life as a prayer. With the addition of representations of the elements, it becomes useful in protecting a child as they sleep. More importantly, it is unobtrusive and does not frighten the child.

 YOU WILL NEED
- ✦ GLASS OF WATER
- ☽ CLEAR QUARTZ CRYSTAL
- ● FEW DROPS OF LAVENDER OIL
- ◗ PINE CONE

METHOD

The articles above represent – in order – water, earth, air and fire, and have several significances in protection spells.

Begin by activating the spell.

Hold the crystal in your hands for a few moments to activate its protective powers.

Do the same with the glass of water.

Drop the crystal into the water and add a few drops of lavender oil.

Visualize your child shielded from all harm.

Hold the pine cone in your hands and ask for its powers of regeneration to be activated.

Place the charged glass and the pine cone together on the bedside table.

Repeat the words:

 Matthew, Mark, Luke and John,
Bless the bed he lies upon
Four corners to his bed,

> Four angels round his head:
>
> One to watch, one to pray,
>
> And two to bear his troubles away!

Obviously, if you have a little girl you should use the words 'she' and 'her'.

Each morning, throw away the water in the glass either down the toilet or outside your door. It is by now 'contaminated' and not for drinking.

Renew the water each night, repeating the rhyme as you do so, and refresh the other objects as you feel necessary.

● If you make the last step of this spell part of the nightly routine, as your child grows up they might like to participate in the actions and words, and should develop a sense of security because of them. If your child has nightmares, use the pine cone as part of your soothing technique by giving it to them to hold.

 To protect a child

By the time a child is about seven years old, they are beginning to venture out into the world away from home, often without either of their parents being present. Teaching your child a simple protection technique is helpful for both you and them. This one is based on Eastern ideas.

 YOU WILL NEED
✦ YOUR CHILD'S IMAGINATION

METHOD

Discuss with your child the best image they can have of protection.

This might be a shield, a cloak, a wall, or perhaps more effectively being surrounded by a cocoon of light.

Working with your child's own visualization image, have them experience what it is like to feel safe and protected.

Agree that whenever they are frightened or under pressure, they can use this visualization.

Then, whenever you have to be separated from your child, repeat these words or similar to yourself three times:

 Forces of light, image of power

Protect [name of child] till we meet again.

Perceive your child surrounded by light, and know that they are as safe as you can make them.

• You may need to reinforce for the child the idea of them feeling protected by an image they have created, but coincidentally you are teaching them to have courage and to experience their own aura and circle of power. You may well find that your parental antennae tend to be alerted quite quickly when your child is having a problem.

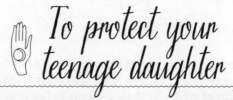

To protect your teenage daughter

This spell arises from ceremonies that honour the Maize Goddess in Mexico. Today, it deals effectively with teenage fears and difficulties, particularly as it honours the maiden aspect of the triple goddess. It is in many ways a rite of passage, and is both a protection and an initiation. It should not be performed unless the girl herself feels that she is ready for such a ceremony.

 YOU WILL NEED
- ✦ WHITE NIGHTGOWN OR SIMPLE DRESS
- ☽ MAIZE BROOM CORN TOPS (SILKS)
- ● 2 OR 4 WHITE CANDLES (OPTIONAL)
- ◖ WATER THAT HAS BEEN BLESSED

METHOD

Traditionally, this ceremony was carried out to cleanse and protect a young girl who had been frightened by inopportune advances, whether human or otherwise.

It is inevitable that teenagers of today will have difficulty in talking about their fears and doubts, but if they can be encouraged to think about them prior to this spell, it is helpful.

The girl should be dressed in the white gown and then lie face downwards with her arms spread outwards in the shape of a cross.

If using candles, place them at her hands, feet or head, or in all four positions.

Do whatever you intuitively feel is right.

'Sweep' her back and legs with the silks, using the blessed water at the same time.

Sprinkle her from head to foot with the water.

Petition the goddess, using words such as:

 Goddess of fertility, power and love

Bless this child here tonight

Protect, guard and guide her as she grows to womanhood

Let her not be troubled by childish fears

But grow to be the woman that she knows she can be.

Next, ask the girl to think about her own future, to take time to imagine and dream about the sort of person she would like to be.

As you sit quietly with her, visualize a white light surrounding her, and ask that she be protected from harm.

At this point, you might wish to make use of the opportunity to encourage her to talk about her dreams and fears, but try not to put pressure on her.

If you have used candles, you can snuff them out, but do not use them for any other magic.

● Hopefully this spell will give your teenager a deeper appreciation of who she is and what she may become. Obviously she must give her consent for what you do together, and this is a time that must be treated sensitively. Knowing that she is protected does not give you licence to take risks, but simply to act responsibly.

New Moon protection

This ritual, which signifies letting go the hurts of the past in a way that allows you to move forward with fresh energy into the future, can be performed at the time of the New Moon. By carrying it out every New Moon, you are gradually able to cleanse yourself of the detritus of the past, often as far back as childhood.

 YOU WILL NEED
- ✦ CEDAR OR SAGE SMUDGING STICK (OR CLEANSING INCENSE)
- ☽ WHITE CANDLE
- ● ATHAME OR RITUAL KNIFE
- ◗ BELL
- ⚡ CAKES AND WINE OR JUICE

METHOD

Cast your circle using the smudge stick or incense to 'sweep' the space as you move around the circle clockwise.

Think of your space as being dome-shaped over your head, and cleanse that space too.

Ring the bell with your arms in the Goddess position (in a 'V' shape above your head), standing with your feet apart.

Say:

 Great Goddess,

Queen of the Underworld,

Protector of all believers in you,

It is my will on this night of the New Moon

To overcome my shadows and bring about change.

I invite you to this my circle to assist and protect me in my rite.

Hold your athame or knife with your hands in acknowledgement of the god (crossed over your chest), with your feet together. Say:

 Great God,

Lord of the Upper Realms,

Friend of all who work with you,

It is my will on this night of the New Moon

To overcome my shadows and bring about change.

I invite you to this my circle to assist and protect me in my rite.

Light the candle, and say:

 Behind me the darkness, in front of me the light

As the wheel turns, I know that every end is a beginning.

I see birth, death and regeneration.

Spend time in quiet thought. If you can remember a time when things have not gone well for you, concentrate on that. While the candle begins to burn properly, remember what that time felt like.

Concentrate on the candle flame and allow yourself to feel its positivity.

Pick up the candle and hold it high above your head. Feel the energy of the light shower down around you, the negativity draining away.

Now draw the power of the light into you and feel the energy in every pore.

Pass the candle around you and visualize the energy building up. If you wish, say:

 Let the light cast out darkness.

You might then wish to perform the protective pentagram from 'Moon wishes' (pages 181–2) to protect you from similar incidents in the future.

Finally, ground yourself by partaking of the food and drink.

Thank the god and goddess for their presence, then withdraw from the circle.

• Cleansing yourself of the past leaves space in your life for new things to happen. Protecting yourself as you do so means you can move forward with positivity.

 *Protection bottle*

The idea behind a protection bottle is that it makes it very uncomfortable for negativity and evil to stay around. As you progress and become more aware, you become more conscious of negativity, while at the same time needing protection from it.

 YOU WILL NEED
* ✦ ROSEMARY
* ☽ NEEDLES
* ● PINS
* ◖ RED WINE
* ⚡ GLASS JAR WITH A METAL LID (A JAM JAR IS IDEAL)
* ◖ RED OR BLACK CANDLE

METHOD

Gather together rosemary, needles, pins and red wine.

Fill the jar with the first three, saying while you work:

Pins, needles, rosemary, wine,

In this witch's bottle of mine

Guard against harm and enmity,

This is my will, so mote it be!

You can visualize the protection growing around you by sensing a spiral beginning from you as its central point.

When the jar is as full as you can get it, pour in the red wine.

Then cap or cork the jar, and drip wax from the candle to seal the top.

Bury the jar at the farthest corner of your property, or put it in an inconspicuous spot in your house.

Walk away from the spot.

• The bottle destroys negativity and evil, the pins and needles impale evil, the wine drowns it, and the rosemary sends it away from your property. This spell works unobtrusively like a little powerhouse, and no one need ever know it is there.

To travel safely

Here, you use more than one correspondence to achieve a safe journey. In this day and age, you can use all sorts of representations to help with this, from protecting your luggage or making the journey pleasant to protecting your person. This spell is divided into separate parts, so you can select whichever sections are appropriate for you.

TO PROTECT YOUR LUGGAGE:

 YOU WILL NEED
- ✦ SPRIG OF ROSEMARY
- ☽ PURPLE RIBBON

METHOD

Place the rosemary inside your suitcase.

Trace the sign of the pentagram over each lock. Weave the ribbon securely around the handle.

Say three times:

 Protected is this case of mine

Return now safely in good time.

- You should recognize your luggage anywhere, but if you do have to lose sight of it – when flying, for instance – it has been made safe and will come back to you quickly. After performing this spell, thieves are unlikely to think your luggage is worth stealing, and it is not likely to get lost either.

PROTECTING YOURSELF PRIOR TO A JOURNEY:

 YOU WILL NEED
- ✦ 4 TEALIGHTS
- ☽ FEW DROPS OF PROTECTIVE OIL SUCH AS SANDALWOOD OR VETIVERT

METHOD

Take a leisurely bath, placing the tealights securely at each of the four corners of your bath.

Add the essential oil to the bathwater.

Visualize all your cares being washed away, and at some point begin concentrating on the journey to come.

Do this without anxiety, just savouring the enjoyment of the journey.

To this end, you might light a yellow candle for communication, and ask that you be open to opportunities to enjoy new experiences, get to know new people and understand the world in which you live.

You can blow the tealights out when you have finished your bath, then relight them when you return home as a thank you for a safe journey.

Next, prepare a charm bag with the following:

 YOU WILL NEED

- ✴ 1 PART BASIL
- ☽ 1 PART FENNEL
- ● 1 PART ROSEMARY
- ◗ 1 PART MUSTARD SEED
- ⚡ PINCH OF SEA SALT
- ◢ CLEAR QUARTZ CRYSTAL
- ◖ COIN OR BEAN, FOR LUCK
- ♥ SQUARE OF INDIGO CLOTH
- ✦ WHITE CORD
- ◗ ADD A REPRESENTATION OF A WHEEL AND/OR A PIECE OF PAPER WITH THE NAME OF YOUR DESTINATION, IF YOU LIKE

Spread the cloth so that you can mix the herbs quickly.

Hold your hands over the herbs and ask for a blessing from Njord the Norse god of travel, or Epona the Horse goddess who accompanied the soul on its last journey.

Gather up the herbs and the representative objects in the cloth and tie it into a bag, making sure it is bound securely with the white cord.

Keep the bag secure about your person.

● You should find that your journey is accomplished without too much trouble, and that people are eager to assist you whenever you need help. You may well find that you are observing more than is usual or are being asked to participate in experiences that might otherwise pass you by.

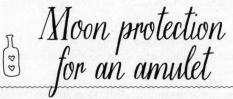

Moon protection for an amulet

This technique can be used to protect an object for use as an amulet – a crystal perhaps, or one of the other amulets listed below. The spell takes in the power from the Moon, and is best done at the time of the Full Moon.

 YOU WILL NEED
- ✦ YOUR CHOSEN AMULET
- ☽ GLASS OF SPRING WATER

 METHOD

Place a crystal or amulet that you regularly carry in the cup of spring water a day before the Full Moon.

The following day, on the evening of the Full Moon, stir the water three times with the fingers of your right hand in a clockwise motion.

Take the cup in your hands and swirl the water around, moving the cup in a clockwise, circular stirring motion three times.

Repeat the following words aloud:

 Oh Light of the Moon

Wrap me

Protect me

Keep me from harm.

Remove your amulet from the cup.

Raise the cup towards the sky, acknowledging the Moon.

Lower the cup, bring it to your lips and drink the water.

Carry the amulet with you until the next Full Moon, in order to ensure full protection.

Repeat this process every month to benefit from the amulet's influence.

When an object has been blessed by the Moon, you enter under her protection, and you symbolically take in her power by drinking the water.

Amulets are seemingly inanimate objects that have been given power by the incantation.

Below are a few amulets that you might like to use:

ANCHOR This represents stability, hope and salvation. It favours all matters relating to the sea, and protects against physical harm.

ANKH (CRUX ANSATA) The Egyptian Cross of Life is the key to the hidden mysteries. It brings about health and abundance and, through knowledge, gives power to the wearer.

ARROWHEAD This gives protection against enemies, bad luck, hexes, jealousy and all negative forces. Placed over your front door (or under the doormat), it deters burglars.

BELLS symbolize angelic forces, the four elements and the cycles of the seasons. They are used to frighten off the Devil and evil spirits.

CASTLES form a strongly protective image. They suggest the doorway to knowledge and power.

COWRIE SHELL This represents prosperity, and when worn by a woman, gives her protection. In Polynesian societies, it was considered a valid form of exchange token.

FAN This is a lunar symbol depicting life unfolding. In Eastern tradition, the fan represents protection and safety.

HAMMER This representation of the formative, masculine principle is particularly powerful in techniques of manifestation (i.e. having something happen). It signifies victory over one's enemies or obstacles, and is especially beneficial for business or career ambitions.

HORSESHOE This is a well-known good luck symbol in many parts of the world. It is often taken to represent the Moon in her crescent form.

KEYS symbolize health, wealth and love. As they both open and close, they also signify birth and death, beginnings and endings, as well as new opportunities and ventures.

KNOT The Celtic Knot is a protective device when worn as an amulet. The Lover's Knot represents perfect union.

OYSTER SHELLS today tend to represent the Moon, because of the association with mother-of-pearl and its luminescence. They protect the wearer from harm.

PINE CONE With its many seeds, this signifies abundance, health, wealth and power. Worn as an amulet or kept within the home, it is said that you will never lack the good things of life.

SEASHELLS are a symbol of femininity, particularly the Mother Goddesses. Signifying birth and regeneration, they represent prosperity and marital bliss.

SUN This represents wealth, health, happiness and fame. It also protects against other people causing you problems.

TORCH This signifies the spark of life, and also illumination and truth.

Every problem perceived
to be 'out there' is really
nothing more than a
misperception within your
own thinking.

Byron Katie

To break a curse

There are various ways to break a curse or a malicious spell. Here you use an object to represent the curse, incense to clear it, and an incantation to deflect it. You then allow natural forces to do their work.

YOU WILL NEED
* SACHET CONTAINING EQUAL PARTS OF:
  * ST JOHN'S WORT
  * LAVENDER
  * ROSE
  * BAY
  * VERBENA
* CLEANSING INCENSE SUCH AS BENZOIN OR DRAGON'S BLOOD
* BLACK CANDLE (TO REPRESENT THE NEGATIVITY)
* WHITE CANDLE (FOR POSITIVITY)
* LEMON
* BOWL OF WATER
* BOWL OF SALT
* YOUR ATHAME OR KNIFE
* GLASS OR CHINA PLATE

METHOD

Light the incense and candles (black on the left, white on the right).

Pass the sachet through the incense smoke, then place it to one side.

Hold the lemon in both hands and allow it to signify the negativity.

Think of all the negative things that have happened and push them into the lemon, particularly if you suspect they are associated with the curse.

Dip your athame or knife in the water, then slice the lemon into three pieces.

Touch each piece of lemon with the tip of the athame or knife.

As you do this, repeat the following:

 Three times three
Now set me free.

Visualize the lemon drawing the negativity away from you and into itself.

As you do this, repeat:

 As sour as this lemon be
Charged and cut in pieces three
With salt and water I am free
Uncross me now, I will it be.

Lemon sour, lemon sour
Charged now with power.

Let this lemon do its task
Its cleansing power I do ask
As this lemon dries in air
Free me from my dark despair.

Uncross! Uncross! I break this curse
But let not my simple spell reverse
I wish no ill, nor wish him [her] pain
I wish only to be free again.

Take each lemon slice and dip it in the salt, making sure it is well coated.

Set the slices back on the altar, and say:

 As it is my will, so mote it be.

Leave the lemon pieces on the altar where they can dry.

Once dry, the spell is complete and the lemon can be thrown away or buried.

If the fruit rots instead, however, you must repeat the spell.

• While waiting for the fruit to dry, keep the sachet with you at all times. It will help to protect you from the effects of the spells and turn away any negativity sent in your direction.

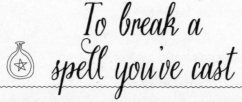

To break a spell you've cast

There are times when we have cast a spell that we should not have done, either because we haven't thought it through or because we have reacted in anger and later realized it was inappropriate. In such cases, we are honour-bound to undo what we have done. This spell is representational, and the best time to do it is after midnight at the time of the Waning Moon.

 YOU WILL NEED

✦ PURIFYING INCENSE SUCH AS BENZOIN OR ROSEMARY
☽ ANGELICA OR ROSEMARY HERBS
● AS MANY WHITE CANDLES AS YOU FEEL IS APPROPRIATE
◗ ROSEMARY OIL
⚡ BEAD FROM A NECKLACE YOU OWN (CLEAR, IF POSSIBLE), OR YOU COULD USE A MUCH-LOVED PIECE OF JEWELLERY OR CRYSTAL IF YOU DON'T OWN A NECKLACE
◗ SMALL SQUARE OF BLACK CLOTH
◖ CORD OR THREAD

METHOD

Anoint your candles with the rosemary oil, working from bottom to top, since you are sending the spell away.

Light the incense and let it burn for a few moments to raise the atmosphere.

Light your candles and as you do so, think very carefully as to why you cast the first spell, what it has caused, and why you wish it removed.

Then say:

🕊️ 🕊️ *Great Mother, I ask a favour of you*

On [date] I cast a spell to [insert type of spell]

I now ask for it to be removed and rendered harmless

May it have no further power or gain.

Place the bead or jewellery and the herbs on the black cloth, and say:

🕊️ 🕊️ *Here I make sacrifice to you, knowing that I must relinquish this object as token of my good intentions.*

Knot the cord around the cloth, saying as you do:

🕊️ 🕊️ *I transfer the power of the spell to this object*

And enclose it within its own darkness

So be it.

Use three knots for finality. Seal the knots by dripping wax on them.

Then take the bag to a source of running water or a clear space, and throw it away as far from you as you can.

If your first spell was done in anger or fear, then say:

🕊️ 🕊️ *Begone anger, begone fear*

It is done.

• You should find that you have got rid of any negativity you have felt. By giving up something that belongs to you, you have cleared yourself of the law of cause and effect, and of any spiritual difficulty caused by your initial action.

The best parts of you
are hidden where you're
most afraid to look.

Michael Benner

Banishing powder

Most herbs can be pulverized either in a pestle and mortar, coffee grinder or blender to make various powders for specific purposes. In an emergency, you can also use commercially dried spices and blend them yourself. The following powder is designed to get rid of pests, both human and otherwise. It has a slightly Eastern feel to it.

YOU WILL NEED

* ✦ EQUAL QUANTITIES OF PEPPERCORNS (BLACK, WHITE, CUBEB, PAPRIKA ETC)
* ☽ SIMILAR QUANTITY OF GINGER
* ● WASABI (JAPANESE HORSERADISH) POWDER

METHOD

Grind all the ingredients together.

As you do so, visualize your pest walking away from you into the sunset.

Sprinkle the resulting powder sparingly around the edge of the area you wish to protect.

You can also sprinkle the powder where you know the pest will walk past.

● There is no need to make it obvious that you have sprinkled this powder. Indeed, the more unobtrusive it is, the better. Since this spell uses the idea of heat – all the ingredients are 'hot' – the powder should not be used when you are angry, and you must be very sure you don't wish to have any contact with your pest.

Pet protection spell bottle

Pets can be particularly sensitive to atmosphere, so if you do a lot of spell work that deals with negativity, it is wise to protect them against being inadvertently contaminated. The herbs and candle in this spell do this very efficiently.

 YOU WILL NEED
- ✦ SMALL JAR OF SOIL
- ☽ SMALL JAR OF SALT
- ● WHITE TAPER CANDLE
- ◗ YOUR BURIN OR STICK PIN
- ⚡ WINE BOTTLE
- ◖ BAY LEAF
- ◖ TABLESPOON OF DILL SEEDS
- ♥ TABLESPOON OF FENNEL SEEDS
- ✦ CARNELIAN STONE

 METHOD

Put half the soil into the bottle. Add half the salt on top of that (to make layers). Add the bay leaf and the dill and fennel seeds. Put the rest of the salt on top of this, and the rest of the soil on top of the salt.

Drop the carnelian stone on top of everything.

Use your burin or stick pin to carve the following on the taper candle:

🪶 *Protect [pet's name].*

Fit the candle into the top of the bottle. If it is too big, wedge it in, or warm the bottom slightly until it stays securely by itself.

Burn the candle when convenient.

You don't have to burn it all down at once, but eventually the candle will burn itself out.

When the candle will not stay lit any longer but forms a plug for the top of the bottle, put the spell bottle near the place where your pet spends most of their time.

● If you are fearful that your pet may be stolen, add a sprig of rosemary to the herbs in the bottle. You can expect to become very aware of your pet's wellbeing in the light of this spell. Any conditions you have not previously noticed may become apparent.

Bast spell

In ancient Egypt, cats were under the protection of the cat goddess Bast, hence they were once seen as witches' familiars. This spell and its invocation link you with that goddess and seek her protection for you and your pet. By wearing an amulet, you can seek the protection of the Lunar Goddess in her many forms.

 YOU WILL NEED

✴ LUNAR INCENSE IN EQUAL MEASURES OF JUNIPER, ORRIS ROOT AND CAMPHOR

☽ 2 WHITE CANDLES

● IMAGE OF A CAT (PERHAPS A CHARM, FIGURINE OR BROOCH)

◗ IMAGE OF BAST (IF YOU CAN FIND ONE)

 METHOD

Light your incense and candles. When ready, invoke the power of the goddess:

 Goddess Bast, Goddess Bast

Mother of Mahes from centuries past

Feline keeper of the Royal flame

Hear me now, as I call your name.

Wise bestower of feminine scents and charm

Let me and mine never come to harm.

Now offer the amulet to her.

Pass it through the smoke of the incense and through the flame of the candles.

Hold it up, and say:

 With this token that I carry

Of your wisdom and your knowledge

Never doubt I will acknowledge

Those who take this path beside me

As we safeguard your sacred memory.

Wear your amulet to remind you of your loyalty to Bast and all she represents.

● Often when you have made a dedication to Bast, you become far more aware of cats and their habits. Frequently you find you have been given a gift of some sort, which acknowledges the link. This might be something you need or an opportunity to do something you have always wanted to do.

Animal protection spell

When we work with Mother Nature, we are often called upon to protect her creatures. These range from our own pets to animals in the wild, and also those animals that have become our totem animals. This spell uses photographs to represent these animals, or alternatively you could use small figurines. The candles are used to focus your energy, and the oil to create a safe environment.

 YOU WILL NEED
- 2 GREEN CANDLES
- WHITE CANDLE
- PICTURE OR FIGURINE OF AN ANIMAL
- PROTECTION OIL
- CONSECRATED SALT AND WATER
- IF PROTECTING A PET, INCLUDE THEIR FAVOURITE TREAT

 METHOD

Light the green candles, being conscious of the conservation issues in regard to your chosen animal.

Light the white candle to represent the particular animal concerned.

Put the photograph under the white candle or place the figurine next to the candle, and say:

Spirit of fire burning bright

Give your protection here this night.

The moon above for this animal dear

Gives shelter and so freedom from fear.

Draw close all spirits of the same

Come hither! Come hither!

Power of the wild and strength so great!

Defend and safeguard this one's fate.

To complete the spell, either give your pet its treat, or scatter the crumbs outside for other animals to enjoy.

● The animals to which you are drawn are believed to be the ones that will protect and teach you in return for your care. By being aware of their needs, you become part of the cycle of nature and of life.

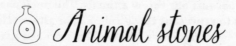 Animal stones

The ancients were very good at perceiving animal shapes in stones and wood, and believed that such shapes could be made to hold the spirit of the animal 'trapped' in such a way. Many artists today are still able to do this, and we too as magic makers can make use of this art. Use any interesting stone or piece of wood you might find.

 YOU WILL NEED
✦ PLEASANTLY SHAPED STONE OR PIECE OF WOOD
☽ PAINTS AND BRUSHES
● DECORATIONS SUCH AS BEADS AND RIBBONS
◐ GLUE OR FIXATIVE
⚡ INCENSE SUCH AS BENZOIN OR FRANKINCENSE
◗ SMALL BOX

 METHOD
Light the incense.

Sit quietly with your object and let it 'speak' to you. Allow ideas to flow as to what it might become – your totem animal, a bear, a horse, or perhaps a dog or cat.

Decorate the object appropriately, taking care to enhance the natural shaping rather than changing it.

Consecrate it in one of two ways: either pass the object quickly through the smoke of the incense three times to empower it with the spirit of the animal; or put it in the box with an appropriate image or herbs, then bury it for three days or place it on your altar for the same period.

This allows the metamorphosis to take place and the spirit of the animal to enter what is now a magical object.

The object is now ready for use, perhaps to help you access the wisdom of the animal, as a healing device or for protection.

● Ancient people believed that the animal object (or 'fetish') had to be fed appropriately to retain its magical powers. Today, corn is an appropriate 'food', as is pollen, although you can use your imagination, since it is your creation. If you don't feed (energize) the fetish for a period, you may need to consecrate it again for it to work properly.

Animal protection collar

A simple way to protect an animal and have it behave well is to braid your own collar for it, to which you can attach various objects. Try to use natural materials wherever possible. Choose the colours of the cords carefully according to the animal's temperament, or to signify the quality you wish the animal to develop – for example, red for a hunting dog, silver for a nocturnal cat, or you may opt for a mixture of three different colours.

YOU WILL NEED
- ✦ 3 PIECES OF CORD SLIGHTLY LONGER THAN THE CIRCUMFERENCE OF YOUR PET'S NECK, TO ALLOW FOR BRAIDING AND TYING
- ◗ SMALL CYLINDER NAMETAG OR A DISC INSCRIBED WITH THE ANIMAL'S NAME AND ADDRESS
- ● SMALL CHARM BAG, ABOUT 3 IN (10 CM) SQUARE, WITH A CORD OR RIBBON TIE
- ◗ SMALL QUANTITY OF CHILD'S CLAY
- ϟ SMALL PIECE OF FLINT
- ◗ SMALL PIECE OF CORAL
- ◖ SMALL CRYSTAL OF ROSE QUARTZ
- ♥ YOUR BURIN
- ✦ PEN

METHOD

Carefully braid the cord while calling on your chosen deity for protection of your animal and weaving in the intention for good behaviour.

Form a rough cylinder from the clay, and before it dries out completely, inscribe it with a protective rune, Ogham Stave or the name of your preferred deity.

Attach the cylinder to the collar you have woven, or place it in the charm bag.

If you are using a cylinder-type pet tag, write the symbol on the back of the paper in the cylinder; if using a circular disc, inscribe it on the back.

Place the flint, coral and rose quartz in the charm bag and attach it to the collar.

Put the collar around the animal's neck, again calling for protection.

• Obviously if your animal is fully grown, you cannot expect a total change in behaviour all of a sudden without additional training. Sometimes an animal needs protection from its own behaviour as much as anything else. This spell gives you a starting point and a foundation from which to continue your work.

If you listen to birds, every day will have a song in it.

Kyo Maclear

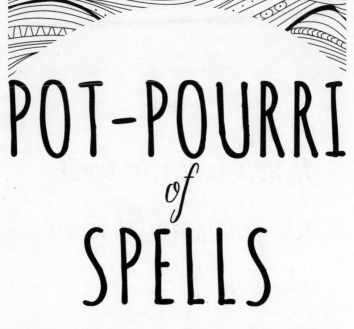

POT-POURRI

of

SPELLS

There are many mindful spells that do not fall easily into the previous categories in this book. A selection is included here so that you may get a flavour of how to widen your perspective and thus further enhance your spell making. In this chapter you will find spells for honouring the directions of the four winds, slowing down a situation, blessing someone moving into a new home, and how to turn your garden into a sacred space.

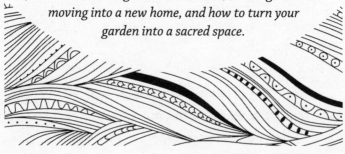

Get rid of a bad feeling

To rid yourself of apprehension when someone is bothering you, or if you find yourself in any situation that is difficult to handle, you can use the power of air to shift it away from you. This spell uses colour to reinforce the magic. Choose a balloon in the more spiritual colours of purple or blue, which works at the highest vibration.

YOU WILL NEED
- ✦ COLOURED BALLOON
- ☽ PIECES OF PAPER
- ● STRING
- ◗ PEN

METHOD

Write on single pieces of paper each problem from which you wish to be free.

Tie them onto the string at regular intervals like a kite tail.

Take everything up to a high place if possible, or a crossroads if not.

Blow up the balloon and tie it securely with the string. As you do so, say:

 As I bind these things together

May I be free of them forever.

Release the balloon into the air and watch it be blown away. As this happens, send it on its way with the following words:

 Spirits of Air and all things good

Take these problems, lift my mood

Give me freedom, give me rest

And let me be what is my best.

Now turn around, walk away and don't look back.

● When you perform this spell, you are allowing the difficulty to be taken away from you. This can be quite a gentle process, usually with little conflict or confrontation.

 # *A statement of intent*

This is not so much a spell as a statement of intent, and is probably best kept private. It should encapsulate a promise you've made to yourself to maximize your potential in every way. Telling someone about your personal undertaking may actually lessen its value and make it seem less attainable. Similar to an affirmation, the statement needs to be short and succinct, so that every time you think about it, it has impact for you.

YOU WILL NEED

✦ AT LEAST 2 PIECES OF PAPER
☽ 2 POSTCARDS
● PEN AND INK (MAGICAL, IF POSSIBLE)

 METHOD

First take a piece of paper and write down as many things as you can think of that you:

> ✦ Want to do.
> ☽ Would like to do.
> ● Feel you ought to do.

(These need not be in the form of an organized list, but can be scribbled down at random.)

Look carefully at each of your statements and eliminate any that seem to repeat themselves.

On another clean sheet of paper, formulate a sentence that, for you, is powerful, meaningful and expresses the repeated sentiment properly.

Do this for each of your core thoughts that become apparent.

With your second sheet of paper, try to reduce the sentences to one very powerful and relevant description of your mission or task in life. Keep this as short but also as forceful as you can.

Keep the two pieces of paper in a safe place for future reference.

The second stage of the exercise is to write out your mission on two postcards.

Place one postcard by your mirror or on your bedside table, where you will see it when you first wake up.

Repeat the statement at least three times as soon as you are awake, and also just before you settle for sleep.

This is so that it is almost the first and last thing that you think about during the day.

Repeat the statement as often as you can during the day, preferably at least three times a day.

Place the other postcard where you can see it in your work area.

With this postcard, remember to move it around so that it does not become 'just part of the scenery'.

Your main personal undertaking contains within it many sub-statements so that, if you wish, you can also concentrate on these sub-statements or change the focus of your main statement to include another aspect.

Because the statement is so personal, it is yours to do with as you will; the only thing you must do is make it work for you.

• Moving the postcard once a week and thinking about the statement reinforces the intent behind it, and gives you the opportunity to change the statement should you so wish. It helps to focus your mind, but also allows the subconscious to 'hear' the intent and to internalize it.

Feelings, whether of compassion or irritation, should be welcomed, recognized, and treated on an absolutely equal basis; because both are ourselves. The tangerine I am eating is me. The mustard greens I am planting are me. I plant with all my heart and mind. I clean this teapot with the kind of attention I would have were I giving the baby Buddha or Jesus a bath. Nothing should be treated more carefully than anything else. In mindfulness, compassion, irritation, mustard green plant and teapot are all sacred.

Thich Nhat Hanh

Four winds spell

This is a herbal spell that honours the four directions. It is easy to do, and simply requires that you know what you want. You can use either a single herb or a number – whichever your intuition tells you. The lists of herbs in the Introduction chapter of this book should give you enough information to make an informed choice. The spell actually works more effectively using dried herbs, since they are better at being scattered to the four winds.

 YOU WILL NEED
- ✷ DRIED OR FRESH HERBS APPROPRIATE FOR YOUR PURPOSE
- ☽ SMALL BOWL OR BAG, TO CARRY THE HERBS

 METHOD

Over about a week, gather the herbs you need.

Mix them together. Quantities and proportions do not matter, as long as you have a large quantity after mixing.

While mixing together, bear your intent in mind.

Put the herb mixture into your bag or bowl, and carry it up to a high place.

Start with the direction that suits your purpose.

Throw a handful of herbs in that direction, saying:

 [Direction] wind, accept now my offering,

Hear my request.

Do the same with the other directions in the same way.

Now spin around at least three times, either throwing handfuls of herbs or allowing them to fall from the bag as you do.

Chant:

 Winds of power, winds so fine,
Bring to me what is rightly mine.

Stand still and allow the world to settle around you.

Give thanks to the elements, then walk away.

● In this spell you are harnessing the element of air, since you are using the wind. The herbs act both as a vehicle for your request and also as a gift to the element of air.

Appealing to St Anthony

This prayer or formula is often used to have a lost object returned to you. In doing the spell, you seek the help of St Anthony of Padua, a Catholic saint of the twelfth century. The incantation is now considered to be a folk remedy, and consists of 'pulling' an object back towards you.

YOU WILL NEED
★ LENGTH OF THREAD OR STRING

METHOD
First, try to remember when you last saw the object.

See it clearly in your mind's eye.

Imagine tying your thread or string to the object. Then go through the motions of pulling it towards you.

Repeat the following words three times:

 Something's lost and can't be found
Please, St Anthony, look around.

You will often get a sense of where the object is. Conversely, you may come across it unexpectedly.

Don't forget to thank St Anthony for interceding on your behalf.

• The words used here are found in similar forms all over the world, clearly demonstrating the link between folk customs and the church. You should not need to use this spell too often if you learn to keep important articles in safe places. That way, when you do need St Anthony's help, it will be readily available.

Pendulum

This is a different method of finding something that you have lost, particularly if it is in the immediate vicinity. The spell utilizes a pendulum, and is a quick way of checking your intuition if you have not yet fully developed your psychic abilities.

YOU WILL NEED

★ PENDULUM, WHICH MAY BE A CRYSTAL ON A SHORT CHAIN, A RING SUSPENDED ON A THREAD, OR A SIMILAR OBJECT

METHOD

Normally, a pendulum is used to answer yes/no questions, but here you take note of the direction in which it swings.

When you have made a link with the lost object either by visualizing it or deciding why you need it, hold the pendulum in your dominant hand and support your elbow on a flat surface.

Allow the pendulum to begin to move, and sense which direction it seems to pull more strongly.

If you are a beginner, repeat the procedure three times.

More often than not, the pendulum will find your object by indicating more than once the direction in which it may be found.

Follow the direction shown, and unearth your object.

• Occasionally an object will disappear completely and not be returned by one of the above methods. It is pointless becoming stressed, since it will reappear in its own good time if you still have need of it. If this doesn't happen, simply consider that the object is subject to spiritual law, which means you no longer require it.

Willow spells

You can use knots to 'fix' a spell – that is, to hold energy to prevent something from happening, or to release energy so that something happens at a chosen time. You may use string or ribbon, or perhaps more effectively, living natural grasses. Willow withies such as those used for basket weaving are good for this type of spell, since willow enhances intuition. Knots enable you to make sure the energy you have directed goes where you want it to go.

 YOU WILL NEED
✦ SHORT LENGTH OF STRING, RIBBON, GRASS OR WITHY

 METHOD

As always, you should be conscious of the fact that it is wrong to try to force someone to do something against their will.

Therefore carefully consider your actions, and be very clear as to why you are trying to influence a particular situation.

In spells where the timing is important, you might prepare the groundwork for success, but tie a knot to keep some control over when the circumstances dictate a proper release.

Let us assume that you have a court case that needs some careful management, and you need to make an impact.

Take your chosen length of material and, as you tie a simple knot, chant words such as:

As this knot is tied in thee

The power is held until set free

'Tis bound, until on my command

The knowledge needed comes as planned.

Put the tied object in your pocket, then – perhaps on the morning of your court case – release the knot at your chosen moment. This will enable you to have all the information and energy you need for a successful outcome.

You can also use this same knot-tying method to enhance your dream content, although the procedure is slightly different.

If you wish to find the answer to a problem in your dreams, after having carefully thought things through as much as you can, hold the withy in your hand and allow your energy to flow into it.

Tie a simple knot while saying:

Catch now my dreams and hold them still

That I may know what is thy will

Create a space that I may see

What answer will be best for me.

Sleep with the tied knot under your pillow, and wait for inspiration.

You may not receive the answer on the first night, so sleep with the knot in place for at least three nights.

● While an answer may not always come in a dream, usually you will find that shortly afterwards the resolution comes about in a flash of inspiration, a certainty of the right action or through information from an outside source. This method ensures that you have received help from both your own inner self and the powers that be.

A chocolate spell

Chocolate was the Aztecs' 'Food of the Gods'. In Mexico it is a required offering during the Day of the Dead, celebrated on November 1st (also known as All Souls' Day) and November 2nd, and can be used to attract those who have passed over. Here it is used as an offering to calm the sacred space and remove the influence of restless spirits.

YOU WILL NEED

- ✦ YOUR ALTAR
- ◗ BAR OF THE BEST CHOCOLATE YOU CAN AFFORD
- ● METAL DISH
- ◗ 4 ELEMENT CANDLES
- ⚡ COPAL INCENSE
- ◗ TEALIGHTS FOR THOSE YOU WISH TO REMEMBER, PLUS ONE EXTRA FOR THE RESTLESS SPIRITS
- ◖ YOUR CAULDRON, FILLED WITH MARIGOLDS

METHOD

Cast your circle, since this is a time when the spirits are abroad.

Light your element candles.

Light the incense to cleanse and sanctify the area, and to draw the spirits home.

Light your tealights except the extra one, remembering each person briefly.

Say:

 I greet my ancestors and loved ones who have gone before me.

Then light the extra tealight, and say:

 I welcome those who wish me well.

Break up the chocolate and put it on the metal plate, keeping one small piece in reserve.

Hold the plate carefully over the tealights until the chocolate begins to soften and perfume the air.

Contemplate what death means to you as you do so. (You may become aware of the presence of the spirits.)

Say:

 Welcome those who share my feast

May those not at rest now be at peace.

Eat your own small piece of chocolate.

Place the plate with the chocolate outside your front door for the spirits to enjoy. Sit quietly as the candles and tealights burn down, and enjoy the sanctuary of your sacred space.

Close the circle when you are done.

• Since the Day of the Dead occurs at the same time as Samhain, this is a suitable way of celebrating and making space within your life for all the good things to come. As you contemplate change and the death of the old, also spare a thought for the life you wish to lead in the year to come.

Sanctifying the Moon

This is a ceremony or ritual that belongs to the Jewish heritage, honouring the New Moon in a very specific way. It is said that the Moon was unhappy with her apparently secondary position in relation to the Sun, and that God placated her with her own special ceremony. While this ritual is addressed to the Moon, it also honours the renewal of the cycle of femininity, and therefore is appropriate for acknowledging the power of the matriarch. We give it here in the form of the old words, since they are so meaningful.

 YOU WILL NEED
★ YOUR VOICE

 METHOD

After the third day of the New Moon, every Jew should salute the Moon with a prayer, either alone or along with their whole congregation.

They should go together to a place where they can see the Moon best, and from there look up at the Moon.

The words to be repeated are:

Blessed art thou, O Lord our God, King of the World,

Who with his Words created the heavens and with the breath of his Mouth the heavenly Hosts:

A Statute and a Time he gave unto them, that they should not vary from their Orders,

They were glad and they rejoiced to obey the Will of their Maker,

The Maker is true and his Works are true.

And unto the Moon, he said that she shall monthly renew her crown and her Beauty toward the Fruit of the Womb

For they hereafter shall be renewed unto her,

To beautify unto their Creator for the Glory of his Name and of his Kingdom

Blessed art thou, O Lord, the Renewer of the Months.

Then say three times:

🪶 *Blessed is thy Former, blessed is thy Maker, blessed is thy Purchaser, blessed is thy Creator.*

Next, rise up onto your toes and say three times:

🪶 *As well I jump towards thee and cannot reach to touch thee, so shall none of mine enemies be able to touch me for harm.*

Then say three times:

🪶 *Fear and Dread shall fall upon them,*

By the Greatness of thine arm they shall be as still as a stone.

As a stone they shall be still by thy Arm's Greatness;

Dread and fear on them shall fall.

The following words should then be said three times to each other:

🪶 *Peace unto ye, unto ye peace, David, King of Israel liveth and subsisteth.*

● This acknowledgement of the Moon's validity was an important part of ancient Jewish thought. The words are not a spell in the true sense of the word, but they are still very potent.

To slow down a situation

When things are happening too fast and we feel that life is running away with us, it is possible to slow things down. For this we use the power of the god Saturn and his control of time, coupled with the idea that if something is frozen, it allows us time to think and consider our actions. We simply make use of everyday articles that are easily available around the home.

YOU WILL NEED
- PAPER
- BLACK PEN AND INK
- ● YOUR FREEZER OR ICE-MAKING COMPARTMENT

METHOD

On the front of the paper, either write a few words or draw a representation of the situation you feel is moving too fast.

On the back of the paper, draw the symbol for Saturn:

Place the paper into your freezer or ice-making compartment, and leave it until you feel you can handle your problem again.

When you are ready, tear the paper into small pieces and flush it away or burn it safely.

● This spell is similar to 'Freeze out' (page 101), except that it uses the power of Saturn, the Roman god of time and agriculture. By using the freezer, we are bringing the spell up to date and utilizing the idea of solidifying something rather than allowing it to flow.

To rid yourself of a problem

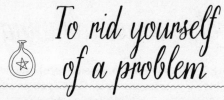

This spell is so simple that it has to work! It is best done at the time of the Waning Moon, and makes use of the elements to symbolize completion.

 YOU WILL NEED
- ✦ OLD SHOE (USUALLY THE RIGHT SHOE)
- ☽ PEN
- ● A FIRE, NATURAL RUNNING WATER OR THE SEA

 METHOD

Write your problem on the sole of your old shoe.

Put the shoe on, then stamp your foot three times.

As you do so, say:

 Begone, troublesome times.

Either throw the shoe into the fire and ensure that it burns properly.

Alternatively, throw the shoe into the stream of water and watch it disappear.

Or throw the shoe into the sea, then walk away.

While any of these events happen, visualize your problem getting smaller and smaller until it disappears.

During this time, inspiration may often come to you as to how you can deal with the difficulty.

● The reason that for using the right shoe is because this is considered to be the more positive and assertive side of the body, which is normally the one needed. If it feels more natural to use the left shoe, however, the result will usually be more passive and non-confrontational.

Cherokee prayer blessing

This blessing is a lovely gift to give to someone when they move into a new home. It is not a spell as such, but produces a special vibration all its own.

 YOU WILL NEED
- ✦ PAPER OR PARCHMENT
- ☽ PEN
- ● INCENSE SUCH AS NINE WOODS INCENSE

 METHOD

Light the incense.

On the paper or parchment, write (or have inscribed if you do not have a steady hand) the following words:

 May the Warm Winds of Heaven

Blow softly upon your house.

May the Great Spirit

Bless all who enter there.

May your Mocassins

Make happy tracks in many snows,

And may the Rainbow

Always touch your shoulder.

Pass the paper or parchment through the smoke three times, then present the gift neatly rolled.

● The Cherokee philosophy is that even the smallest drop of Cherokee blood makes one a Cherokee. While few people can lay claim to such ancestry, we can nevertheless share the awareness that we are all interrelated.

Feast of divine life

All agrarian societies celebrate harvest time – the time of abundance. The Egyptian 'Feast of Divine Life' celebrated the Moon and the belief that it provided the Waters of Life. Nowadays, we recognize the cycle of life and the wheel of the cosmos as it turns. We can still honour the Triple Goddess in all her forms – Maid, Mother and Crone – as was done of old. At the time of the harvest, she is honoured more as the fertile mother.

 YOU WILL NEED
- GREEN CANDLE
- YELLOW CANDLE
- CAULDRON
- WAND
- 3 SYMBOLS OF A FRUITFUL HARVEST (E.G. BREAD, APPLES ETC.)

 METHOD

Prepare your sacred space as usual, including your altar, and say:

The harvest is now done

A peaceful winter lies before us

Dark and light strike a balance

Thanks be to the Triple Goddess.

Light the two different-coloured candles.

Carrying the candles, move clockwise around the ritual area, commencing and completing in the east.

At each cardinal point, pause and say:

Triple Goddess, bless the year's harvest that I bring.

Place the candles safely on the altar, still alight.

Tap the cauldron three times with your wand, and place the symbols in the cauldron.

Say:

 Life brings death, brings life

The wheel of the cosmos turns never-ending

The negative is replaced by the positive.

I honour the Triple Goddess

Harvesting my thoughts

I honour the Triple Goddess.

Meditate for as long as feels comfortable, then close the circle.

● When you have finished, be sure to share the harvest with others of the goddesses' creatures. You might like to bury the apple near an apple or fruit tree as an offering, throw the bread to the birds, or scatter the herbs (if you have used them) on waste ground.

A spell for the garden

If you have your own garden, it is a nice idea to acknowledge the four directions and make the area as much a sacred space as you can. You can do this by using the correspondences of the four elements. Once the garden is blessed, the space can be used for any of the Sun, Moon and nature rituals you find appropriate.

 YOU WILL NEED
- ✦ COMPASS
- ☽ GARDEN FLARES OR CITRONELLA CANDLES TO REPRESENT FIRE
- ● SOLAR FOUNTAIN OR BIRDBATH TO REPRESENT WATER
- ◖ WIND CHIMES OR CHILD'S WINDMILL TO REPRESENT AIR
- ⚡ SMALL COLLECTION OF STONES AND PEBBLES TO SIGNIFY EARTH

METHOD

Consecrate the objects according to the method for 'Consecrating altar objects' (page 32).

Place the objects in the correct positions, asking for a blessing as you place each one.

You might call on the spirits of the elements, the nature spirits or your best-loved deity.

Stand in the middle of your garden, raise your arms, and say:

 Gaia, Gaia, Mother of all

Bless this ground on thee I call

Make it safe for all within

Peace and tranquillity may it bring.

Or you may use your own words, if you wish.

Spin around three times to seal the energy, then sit on the ground and appreciate the newfound energy in your garden.

● If you have very little space, we suggest that you combine all of the elements in a terracotta solar fountain and place it in the east. Terracotta represents earth, the solar aspects suggest fire, the fountain water and the east the element of air.

To give encouragement

**This is a spell that enables you to work with someone
without them necessarily knowing what you are doing.
It is used only for positive encouragement, or to let
someone know that you care about them and what they
do. Anything else will rebound on you threefold.**

YOU WILL NEED
- ✦ JADE, ROSE QUARTZ OR AMETHYST CRYSTAL
- ☽ FRANKINCENSE OR ONE OF THE BLENDS SUITABLE
  FOR THE PURPOSE
- ● OIL BURNER

METHOD

Light the burner.

Pour a little additional oil into your hand and rub your
hands together to raise power.

Hold the crystal in your dominant hand, then pass it three
times through the fumes from the oil burner.

Face the direction where you know the recipient to be.

Say:

Goddess of Love, Goddess of Power,

Hear me now as I thee implore

Help [name] to do what they must

Create the conditions for their success.

Build up a mental ball of energy around the crystal until it
is as powerful as you can make it.

Place the crystal by the side of your bed, directing the
energy of the ball towards the recipient, knowing that
the energy will be transmitted as self-confidence for the
task at hand.

Visualize the person concerned standing tall and confident in a shaft of light stretching from the crystal to them.

Next morning, wash the crystal under running water.

Store the crystal until it is needed again, or give it to the person concerned.

• This spell works because you have no expectations. Your gift of encouragement is freely given, without thought of reward. The payoff comes when you see the recipient succeed in their own way.

Conclusion: So let it be

There are so many spells available across so many disciplines that it is almost impossible to do justice to them all. Spell making is such an individual craft, according to one's own beliefs, that nobody can or indeed should be so bold as to try to tell others what to do, unless there is an accepted pupil–teacher relationship in place. It is only possible to give guidelines. For this reason, if a spell doesn't work for you in the way that it has been given in this book, do try it again on another occasion, and use your intuition to decide what might be changed or adjusted to suit your own personality.

The actions taken during the process of spell making really become so individual that only you yourself know what you actually did to make a particular technique work. For this reason, spell making is one of the few occupations that is truly creative in its output. You are never quite sure what the end result is going to be. You really do have the ability to make things happen, and it is said that: "A handful of skill is better than a bagful of gold." Someone else might do exactly the same thing as you, but possibly get a totally different result.

Finally, this book is really no more than a kindergarten primer. It contains a number of spells garnered from many sources, some very different to our own preferred way of working, and we are therefore very grateful to those people who have made their information available. We would hope that the book will pique your curiosity so that you take your own mindful studies further. As you search for knowledge both esoteric and otherwise, bear in mind that there are some constraints on the use of spells. You should never use them deliberately to wish ill towards someone – this will only rebound on you at some stage of your life. You need to take full responsibility for what you do, so think very carefully and always be aware of what you do.

With all of this in mind, we leave you with an old Irish blessing:

May love and laughter
   light your days,

And warm your heart and home.

May good and faithful friends
   be yours,

Wherever you may roam.

May peace and plenty bless
   your world,

With joy that long endures.

May all life's passing seasons

Bring the best to you and yours!

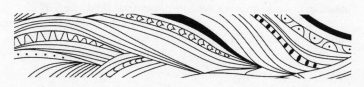

Index